INTELLIGENT DESIGN   DAMAGED EMOTIONS

Biblical Inner Healing

BLACK HOLE OF DEPRESSION

PAST LIFE ISSUES   BROKENNESS

by Mike Mendoza

GATEWAY PRESS
A Division of Aion Group Multimedia
and Gateway International Bible Institute

BIBLICAL INNER HEALING
ISBN# 978-0-9915657-5-7
Cover Photo: Albund

Published by:

GATEWAY PRESS
A Division of Aion Group Multimedia
and Gateway International Bible Institute

20118 N 67th Ave
Suite 300-446
Glendale, Arizona 85308
www.aionmultimedia.com

Copyright © 2014 Mike Mendoza. Printed in the United States of America.
No part of this publication may be reproduced, stored in a retrieval system, or transmitted in any form or by any means – electronic, mechanical, digital photocopy, recording, or any other without the prior permission of the author.

All rights reserved solely by the author. The author guarantees all contents are original and do not infringe upon the legal rights of any other person or work. No part of this book may be reproduced in any form without the permission of the author. The views expressed in this book are not necessarily those of the publisher.

TABLE OF CONTENTS

CHAPTER ONE: BIBLICAL PSYCHOLOGY VS. SECULAR PSYCHOLOGY   1

CHAPTER TWO: SEPARATION FROM GOD IN WESTERN CULTURE   4

  Rebuilding Credibility   6

CHAPTER THREE: RELIGION AND PSYCHOLOGY   12

  The Enlightenment   15

  The Hand and Voice of God   17

  The Perennial Philosophy   19

  Three Steps of The Fall   20

  The Stages in the Circle   20

  Gender - Depending on Your Worldview   23

  The Law of Love   26

  The Health Problem   26

CHAPTER FOUR: THE FIVE DECISIONS TO BE WELL   29

  Decision #1 - The Faith Decision   32

    The Risk of Being Teachable   33

    Come Let Us Reason   35

    Point of Freedom   36

  Decision #2 - The Dependency Decision   36

    What Are Feelings and Emotions?   40

    Where Do Feelings Come From?   40

Responding To The World	42
Point of Freedom: Understanding The Dynamics of Dependency	43
Decision #3 - The Personal Responsibility Decision	45
Responding To The World	47
Boundaries for Freedom - The Discovery of Freedom	48
Decision #4 - The Morality Decision (Morality Law and Purpose for Life)	49
Responding to the World, Moral Order - Trusting the Hand of God	51
Point of Freedom	51
Decision #5 - The Faith, Love, and Hope Decision (The High Ground of the Kingdom Plateau)	52
Responding To The World - The Higher Ground	55
What is Love?	55
Point of Freedom	56
Putting The Five Decisions to Work	57

CHAPTER FIVE: THE GROWTH OF PERSONAL FREEDOM 59

Five Levels of Repentance	60
Truth	60
Dependency	61
Personal Responsibility	61
Obedience	62
Faith, Love and Hope - The Kingdom Plateau	62

Parenting and Children 64

Some Diagnostics Help - Moral and Spiritual Inventory 67

Track Record 68

Moving From Discipleship Into Healing 70

The Three Meanings of Faith 71

Four Decisions of Faith 73

Faith and Operational Truth - The Gap Between Appearance
and Reality 75

CHAPTER SIX: THE DAMAGED SOUL 77

The Deepest Damage 79

A Picture of the Damaged Soul 79

Metaphysics, Feelings and Relations 83

Once Burned, Twice Shy 85

The Three Steps Into The Fall 88

Disintegration of The Soul 89

CHAPTER SEVEN: REALITY VS. FREUD 92

The Unholy Alliance and The Failure of The Cork: Un-Whole
and Unholy 93

The Holy Alliance, The Faith Commandment and Childing ... 96

The Problem, Healing and Commonsense 103

Why An Unconscious? 104

Relying and Attending - A Distinction Between "Attend To" and
"Rely Upon" 108

Mothering and Being 110

Archetypal and Concrete ... 111

Objectifying the Unconscious ... 112

CHAPTER EIGHT: BUILDING SELFHOOD WITH THE FIVE DECISIONS ... *114*

The Friendly Unknown ... 116

Conscious Precedes Unconscious ... 116

Light At The Bottom ... 117

Maturation and Personal Relation With Our Creator ... 117

Two Levels of the Unconscious ... 118

Keeping Things Together ... 119

Personal Truth at the Core of Life ... 123

Split and Collapse ... 124

The Pit of Unreality ... 126

A Warp In the Human Psyche ... 127

The Root of the Tree ... 130

Letting Go and Letting God ... 132

The Five Decisions ... 135

Six Things That Destroy The Unconscious Realm: ... 137

Incarnation and Reality ... 138

Intellect, Imagination and Story Telling ... 139

God and Gender ... 141

CHAPTER NINE: INCARNATE AND IMAGINABLE ... *144*

Personal Relationship With God ... 145

Laying The Foundation For Walking With Jesus	149
Pebbles and Drops	149
The Healing of Relationships	150
Starting the Walk With Jesus	151
Transferring Dependency	152
Wimpy Jesus	153
The Healing - Three Sets of Parents	154
Sanctification	156
The Possible and The Real	156
The Long Ago Good	158
Metaphysical Grace	159

CHAPTER ONE: BIBLICAL PSYCHOLOGY VS. SECULAR PSYCHOLOGY

What makes us tick; why are we out of sync? We have a good intellectual life but a bad emotional life. For instance, if there are two persons in us fighting to make sense, there is no unity. On one hand we are growing well, but on the other we are not.

Psychology is looking inside of yourself to see all the bad things. This self-discovery is needed because, as Christians, with all the teaching and growth programs, we lack joy and peace. We don't experience ourselves as children of God, even in Christian fellowship. Out in the world the presence of God in us "evaporates."

It is disappointing that the healing ministry is only a small part of the Christian teaching and preaching. Christian counseling does not relate the healing process to our relation with Jesus Christ. Christians have handed over their healing to secular physicians, psychiatrists and psychologists and psychology has become a substitute for religion. The church ignores the healing ministry because they don't believe in it.

If you integrate honest biblical faith with honest psychological studies, is this considered to be from the devil? The suspicion that psychology is evil and opposes faith in God is untrue to the Bible because faith and reason go together. The only effective psychology is in the Bible. The meaning of "psychology" is to deal with the mind (mental processes, human behavior, personal actions, human traits, characteristics and thoughts). The hardest and deepest problems are not resolved by psychology, but only by God.

The secular study of the psyche beyond the natural (or known) mind is a good thing when done in an honest desire for truth. However, the biblical study of the soul is religious and secular studies are limited in this area. We all face vital issues like questioning the stability and meaning of life. "Can I be loved for who I am and not for what I do?" If therapists included God in their psychology, they would bear much fruit.

Humans tend to be autonomous, independent and self-governing, and psychology can't explain why because it's a spiritual sin problem. The biblical view can incorporate the truth found by secular research, and facts found by secular research about the psyche (unknown world of a person - their mind) can also be incorporated to the biblical view and make better sense of it. Many things religious people discover share no common ground with secular studies. Secular psychology can't deal with the meaning of life, moral standards, and guilt (which are all important to our psychological studies) because they leave God out.

The Bible, together with biblical inner healing, has the resolutions for the problems of the human race.

1. Faith has to make sense and relate to everyday life. The Bible is commonsense. Once you believe it, it mind-bogglingly answers mysteries and the unexpected. God is a God of reason and order, not of intellectual, emotional or spiritual chaos. Only God has the highest understanding because He is all-knowing.

2. The truth is not the domain of the "experts." The experts don't get to heaven by their expertise. Biblical theology has been researched and understood by the ordinary mind. The Gospel is

commonsense, and this includes the Judeo-Christian world view. You don't need an education to understand that the gospel makes you healthy.

3. Is spiritual truth sacramental, related to this world of space and time? The invisible, spiritual things are part of the physical material also. The physical manifests the spiritual. God created us in His image; did God create the heavens and the world also in His image? Does everything we see have God's imprint? Is it seen as sacramental or created by Him?

CHAPTER TWO: SEPARATION FROM GOD IN WESTERN CULTURE

The Genesis account of creation, (the Judeo-Christian account) is biblical in saying that the entities (humans) are persons; not atoms, molecules, essences or abstractions. The values of life are personal relationships. As stated by the first and second commandments, our primary relationship is with God, and our secondary relationship is with each other. Our brokenness and wholeness have to do with holiness.

The Western civilization is Christian, and identified by its science and civil laws which are rooted in the biblical worldview. The Christian civilization has rejected it; the secular world has secularized it, and it has affected the Christians.

America is barely reproducing itself. Like Europe, it is eroding from within, killing 1 out of every 4th child and replacing them with illegal immigrants. It is also eroded by liberal democracy, pagan sexuality and attacked by Islam while the divided Christian Community shows no interest.

The driving forces in secular (or pagan) society are pleasure, power, and pride. Any culture that does not submit to God will disappear. Why should a rational human being believe or listen to anything that would destroy them? The god of this secular world has blinded him.

Deeper than any culture in history, Westerners have depersonalized their world (and themselves) by becoming numb and calloused to the spiritual world. "Children are not being challenged to be creative and to adapt to life. We are a nation of wimps, becoming fragile with anxiety and depression, having no identity, and with no sense of accomplishment or happiness. In the 90s, this surpassed people over age 40." (C. Rosen p. 34)

Some no longer want to be creatures of the Creator, but want to be the creators. They are living in denial because dependency on God and obedience to Him doesn't make sense to them. They would rather be independent, self-governing, morally self-sufficient, believing that technology will make their day. In Genesis 3: 4-5, the serpent didn't tell Adam and Eve, "In the day you eat of it [the tree of knowledge] you shall die." He said, "You shall be like God." So we become what we worship; depersonalized, numb, insensitive to personhood, far from community life of sharing without healthy interdependence. We don't know how to love our neighbor as we love ourselves. Neighborhoods in America don't exist anymore. Secularism has attacked the biblical foundation of the Western Civilization.

A newly discovered psychological tool that is used in the school system is called "mind control." Christians have their tails between their legs and are losing the battle in the 19th century going into the 20th century. The secular world has taken over the scientific and the civil law arenas and have weakened the Christians because they don't want to have anything to do with it.

We have become a nation of "soft males."[1] We have no stomach for spiritual warfare. The world has depersonalized our personhood and we have become what we worship. Secularized science is demoralizing; disintegrating our nature as persons. There are no spiritual or public leaders or politicians that confront the homosexuality agenda. Christians are forgetful, unmindful, unaware and unarmed in the spiritual battle that's waging on. The

---

[1] Bly, Robert. *Iron John: A Book about Men*. Reading, Mass. : Addison-Wesley, 1990. Print.

Western civilization is wielding a rubber sword with its pants around its knees. Men who are supposed to protect their families send their wives to the abortion clinic or to the military. [2]

When we are free to seek truth and righteousness, things work. Our lives don't work when we think like the world or when we don't ask ourselves if our life is working and think that we don't have to fix it. It is the new "reality-based" culture, imagining ourselves into our own cosmic tomb; a depersonalized world which eats up persons. (Psycho-Historical Reality).

Rebuilding Credibility

Christianity alone can save the world from self-dissolution. Spiritual renewal and renewal for understanding God to know that we are made in His image requires renewed understanding of our human nature. Ending the 20th century, the Christian's intellectual and artistic renewal grew and was steadily converting the world. Going into the 21st century, Christian credibility fell, causing a fall of morals in the West. Christians are a long way from capturing the intellect, imagination and spirits of Westerners. The lack of Christianity results in a sinful culture that breeds sinful people.

Christians are spiritually, intellectually and emotionally healthy because we obey God. We can transform a sinful culture. A sinful culture does not know how to raise stable, capable, and free persons; only God can. However, Christians have abandoned God in the public arena, and are unable to explain how we know the truth of the Christian faith and Gospel. Because of this we are ignored. There is a need to recover our biblical understanding of human nature. By doing so, our spiritual credibility will be recognized because the image of God is stable and unchanging. We who are made in His image are also stable. Christians make the best scientists because we believe in creation.

---

[2] Kirkland Roe vs. Wade. U. S. Supreme Court. 1973. *Justia US Supreme Court*. N. p. , n. d. Web. <http: and and supreme. justia. com and cases and federal and us and 410 and 113 and case. html>.

Christians have handed over science to the secular world because we refuse to be involved. Because of this, we have lost the battle for modernity out of an interest to only be "Christian" and seek the truth in all areas. It is a steady erosion of the biblical worldview and the Judeo-Christian credibility, thanks to the secular people. If the secular worldview takes over, Christianity will drift into strict legalism that will cause us to lose our biblical roots and fall into the world's system.

Isaiah 1:18 KJV, "Come now, and let us reason together, saith the Lord: though your sins be as scarlet they shall be white as snow..." The Gospel is of interest to all, not just Christians, and can answer the universal questions they have. Any person can investigate Jesus, who promised us to take us to the Father.

The biblical worldview on the story of Creation and Judeo-Christianity is opposed by the secular pagan worldview. The biblical worldview of the sexuality and gender of man and woman are both made in the image of God. The other view by the secular and pagan perspective is that they are not made in God's image. We have to be cautious in defining doctrinal standards, because some people are offended if we don't share their beliefs. Those traditions are a gift of God, because they come from our forefathers. We must have full use of our reasoning powers in our search for the truth and understanding who God is. The Spirit of God ignores the different beliefs of the church and various denominations, because the true church will combine it in a Godly order. Ecclesiastes 4:12 states that, "A threefold cord is not quickly broken."

Romans 12:2 says, "Be transformed by the renewing of your mind." The transformation of the mind is not only intellectual, we also have to explain why we believe what we believe. If we can't explain it, the secular world will ignore us and we will lose our intellectual credibility.

God is reality and only offers reality. Our wholeness depends on our reality contact with Him and we need to learn how to identify it. The Judeo-Christians of the Western culture are retreating into the Dark ages of uncivilized Neo-barbarism. We need inner spiritual fortitude to face the counterfeit and lies of relative truth, inclusive of pseudo-pluralism inside and outside the Church. In order to do this we need emotional and spiritual stability, to be forgiven, healed, and be well-educated Christians. Christian Psychology and inner healing are needed because we become a corked up and "bottle-up" part of our self when we can't tolerate the presence of someone or when we protect something.

The yearning for a free sense of selfhood comes by inner healing. Inner healing is reliving the bad situation or bad circumstance that create trauma. Imagine reliving a past memory; remember the place, who was there, what they did to you... can you feel the emotional atmosphere? It was a hard time in your life when part of you got shoved down into your bottle. Remember how you felt being there? If, this time, Jesus walked up to the situation, how would you feel? Better? Nothing is impossible for Him. How would the other person (demon image) feel? Bad? I would introduce Jesus to him and tell him that Jesus told me to forgive him. The demon image, bad image figure of that thing bottled-up inside of me, would be shocked and flee. I would be healed and be set free.

Therapy (or "healing of memories") is known as inner healing, the discovery of healing using the imagination of the human personality. Biblical inner healing is getting one's spiritual life together with one's emotional life. "The healing of memories" is walking back with Jesus into a memory and being healed of that memory. Inner healing needs to be distinguished from spiritual maturity, formation and spiritual direction. "Spiritual direction is help given from one Christian to another, to pay attention to God and to respond to God, to grow in intimacy with God. This spiritual direction is based on Christian experience, not religious ideas, spiritual direction is different from moral guidance."[3] The imagined wall (worldview) between secular "psyche" and the "spiritual soul"

---

[3] Barry, William A. , and William J. Connolly. *The Practice of Spiritual Direction.* New York: Seabury, 1982. Print.

vanishes. In the Biblical world there is no distinction between soul and psyche. Psychologist are dealing with souls without God. This is a disadvantage because its a secular worldview.

When your spiritual maturation, prayer, worship and Bible study are not working, it's because of inner emotional issues, and inner healing is needed. We have a "bottle of repression" inside of us into which we stuff our unwanted feelings and emotions with a cork on it. Part of ourselves is imprisoned in that bottle unable to function with the rest of ourselves yearning to get out.

The presence of the Holy Spirit (the comforter) is healing and gives us abundant life. God made our human nature and wants to heal us. We need to learn all we can about it to cooperate with the healing, that's what biblical psychology is about. We learn about God because we are made in His image and we learn about ourselves.

Spiritual healing is when we focus on Jesus. This is Judeo-Christianity. The West is Judeo-Christian, and our Christianity and Christian theology comes from the Jewish Torah. Biblical psychology rests on the biblical worldview that humans are modeled from the image of God. We are planned by a personal Creator by intelligent design and life, growth, and healing are about our relationship with God. The Primitive Church believes that God heal us when we have a relationship with Him and that our healing is not separate from one spiritual life. This was also true with early paganism, philosophy, psychology and religion; they all agreed on this.

Secular attitudes arose in the Middle Ages during the Renaissance (Europe's Enlightenment) in an explosion of art, literature and learning. During this Enlightenment, modern secularism was the triumph of the impersonal cosmos of paganism over the personal cosmos of the Bible. Evolution was diverting and overshadowing the Enlightenment and science in the personalist biblical framework. There was a split between the sacred and the irreligious secular. The bridge between Christians and Secularists collapsed into a chasm, both into a fortress mentality. The Enlightenment is commitment to reason. It was not secular; it came by intellectual ferment in the Middle Ages. By the discovery of ancient Greek philosophy, which contributed valuable intellectual tools, this Hellenic culture had a pagan worldview which is destined to fail[4]. Science started as a biblical event, not secular or pagan. Christians became frightened when the secular intellectuals tried to prove them wrong. They backed off, and science and the Enlightenment became secular.

After the Reformation, failure by the Christians to sustain an intellectual defense on foundational religious issues led to religious wars, causing many to reject Christianity. Christians refusing to discuss or defend their views in public sabotaged the real biblical enlightenment. God has given His people both science and civil law as a gift, but Christians have built walls between themselves with politics and science.

Reason and revelation are the two edges of the Sword of the Spirit. Since the world "loved darkness rather than light", the Christians have retreated, left open the public arena and refused to explain their beliefs by going into the shadows. This helped the emerging Secularism, which is based on "impersonalism" of the Greek philosophical worldview taken over by them. The rejection of the biblical doctrine of Creation and Hellenic thought patterns accepted by Christians caused havoc to the personal foundation of biblical theology.[5] The Christians in accepting the philosophical tools developed by Greek philosophers, imported impersonal worldview bringing havoc to the Christian theology.

Science had biblical roots and also Hellenic thought tools. Science was used by the Secular more effective than by the Christians in the spiritual warfare of the developing "modern" era. The scientific way became that of proving the irrelevance or non-existence of God. The problem was not science but the scientists.

---

[4] Murray, Gilbert. *Five Stages of Greek Religion*. Garden City, NY: Doubleday, 1955. Print.

[5] Pearcey, Nancy. *Total Truth: Liberating Christianity from Its Cultural Captivity*. Wheaton, IL: Crossway, 2004. Print.

Evolution is just an incorrect, alternative explanation for life's existence that does not disprove the biblical explanation. Evolution's rise was only emotional and spiritual, but not intellectual. Science developed in Europe at the end of 1000 years of a culture that was saturated in Christian thinking, belief and practice. Science did not develop in opposition to the biblical worldview, it required the biblical view of life to develop.

CHAPTER THREE: RELIGION AND PSYCHOLOGY

Some Christians believed that healing came only from secular psychotherapists. They were told that their Christian belief was only an illusion and that real healing does not require belief in God. We must free the human race from the negative power of secular morality. "Inferiority, guilt, fear and sin comes because of morality which is the concept of right and wrong. Psychiatry must get rid of good and evil."[6] In other words, get rid of religion so that the new religion psychotherapy takes its place.

In 1962 prayer is banned in the public schools, causing the American culture to fall. In 1973 abortion is legalized. Psychiatry and its usage of drugs have caused many to be additive, in an easy way out, a quick fix, rather than dealing with the spiritual and moral issues. Those seeking inner peace and well-being apart from God will not find it in psychotherapy; it only comes from God. The joy of life is only found in a Spirit-filled Church.

The biblical tradition of the cosmos can't mix with Eastern religions. If they mix, biblical traditions will be distorted. There

---

[6] Faber, Dorothy A. , ed. Editorial. *Christian Challenge* n. d. : n. pag. *The Christian Challenge*. Foundation For Christian Theology. Web. <http: and and www. challengeonline. org and >.

are things discovered by the secular that can be used by Christians because truth is truth no matter where it appears. There have been many helpful discoveries, but Christians have been too judgmental of them.

The secular error is in thinking they have the answer to sin and brokenness, not God. If God is not in the center of a person's life, it will not work. Life is like a puzzle and often the missing piece is God. In all of human history, more healing miracles are seen today because they are not extraordinary but ordinary. Jesus considered a relationship with God ordinary.

There are two ways at looking at the world; the biblical way and the philosophical way. Hinduism from Eastern religions has been coming into the Western civilization.[7] Christians focus on the fallenness of things (which is the doctrine of salvation) and not on the creation doctrine in fulfilling the mandate to have dominion over the world. The "fundamentalist" liberal Christian can't distinguish the Godly from the worldly or God from the world, rejecting anything too "biblical." Science could not have happened without a biblical culture. [8]

We live in a personal world that is people-friendly. God made us in His image and with a purpose. Biblical psychology knows the human nature in biblical terms. Biblical psychology is rooted in biblical theology and anthropology. Biblical psychology from a biblical point of view is a description of the soul, how it works and how it needs God. The Bible's view of human nature includes the unconscious and how our sexual natures surpasses what the world offers. The Bible is not philosophy nor psychology, but gives us a cosmic picture of both of them. Biblical psychology is not a "do it yourself religion" nor is it a "quick fix." It is the

---

[7] Huxley, Aldous. *The Perennial Philosophy*. N. p. : Fontana, 1958. Print.

[8] Jaki, Stanley L. *Science and Creation: From Eternal Cycles to an Oscillating Universe*. New York: Science History Publications, 1974. Print.

healing of memories, helping persons damaged by a destructive dependency as in a parent-child relationship. Those unhappy memories we can't tolerate, we tend to stuff and bottle-up, repress them, but they will come back to haunt and plague us, warping and twisting our attitudes and behaviors.

When we "stuff" a memory, part of ourselves gets stuffed also. A little child in me gets trapped on the inside. The adult in me does not know how to handle that child and the child may feel terror, fear, rage or rebellion against adult and parental figures. The child is locked in a self-made prison. If that bad-image child does not come out, I will never experience myself as a child of God. I by myself can't get that child out, who will set the child free and open the cork so I can be what God wants me to be? If this bad memory doesn't come out, I will try not to be a child of anybody but be my own independent, autonomous decision-maker.

There are two fundamental areas of psychology; the unconscious and human sexuality. Sex and gender issues are in our memories because we were mothered and fathered by our parents. We are psycho-sexual and also psycho-gender. Miracles are thought to be rude intrusion into the world of nature. Healing in the Kingdom is expected. The first miracle was not separate from nature, it is the very creation of nature. Redemption means making nature work right which was intended in the first place.

"Liberalized" Christian therapy is secular therapy. Biblical psychology is Christian therapy. It is healing a person who has a personal faith relationship with God and for healing of our feelings, emotions and relationships. Your relationship with God will make you feel and accept others and you will perceive the world with love. Biblical psychology is cooperating with God to make things right and learning how the human nature works. God designed the human nature as part of the world and we learn to cooperate with God in that plan. Inner healing does not happen independently of the nature of our world. We live with our human nature in a cosmos that has its own structure and nature.

The Enlightenment

In the last four centuries, science has advanced and the modern man discovered the nature of the cosmos without God. America was founded on biblical principles. In the 1850s the biblical enlightenment principles were secularized by the French Revolution and had taken root in America, affecting its biblical roots. Christians are not capable of sharing their faith in public and have lost their courage to stand for truth. They have become soft males.

The secular attempt to use reason that justifies rebellion against God is based on the serpent's promise that they will "be as God." In the latter 1900's, The Enlightenment infiltrated and damaged America's biblical roots with secularized psychology by brainwashing the minds of students and Christians. Those that invented this psychology created a monster, causing damage to many and to themselves. Some of them repented in their later writings for forming students into independent autonomous, decision-makers. The "Hierarchy of needs" are the levels of needs we have as we mature into "self-actualized" independent, autonomous, decision-makers and self-made men. This secular psychology is helpful but without God it's destructive. A psychology that says that God is not needed or does not exist is destructive. This new wisdom teaches the human animal how to be "happy" not "moral," how "to feel good" but not to "relate well."[9]

The hope that people looked for failed in secular psychology, which is the study of human nature, its frustration and broken relationships. What has this new wisdom done? In addition to mental hospitals and therapies that work for awhile, two world wars cultural disintegration from the 60's to the 21st Century. This "Enlightenment" without God has people in a black hole of frustration. A life that is undisciplined by the law and the grace of God will not work. If the biblical worldview is correct, then the Godless knowl-

---

[9] Maslow, Abraham H. *Hierarchy of Needs: A Theory of Human Motivation.* N. p. : www. all-about-psychology. com, 2011. Print.

edge of the cosmos has led the world out of control. The "Enlightenment" has led us into a new Dark Age.

We live in the world that's comfortable and pleasurable, but not truthful, righteous or loving. Truth, righteousness and love are not part of the Western mindset. We live in a pathological world that breeds pathological people because we ate the forbidden fruit. We live in a sinful world as God said we would; a world that leads us to death. False ideas can mislead whole cultures and whole generations, but true ideas can cause growth and stability of people and cultures.

Contemporary Western culture does not use its head. The people think only on feeling good and things that are pleasurable. When a problem comes they don't know what to do. There is a "philosophical depression" over the meaninglessness of life, an inability to find a reason to live in the stress of life. The fallen system of this world has contributed to this depression. Healthy babies who are never touched or cuddled give up on life and die, and the same stands with older people. The world has lived off the many prior blessing of God in past years, but those blessings are about to run out, because of their attempts at the Godless "Enlightenment" and the failure of Christians to feed new spiritual capital blessing into their culture. We live in a dark universe and world to where there are casinos with its gambling and bright lights, where there are drugs, sexual promiscuity, bars, and high-adventure sports (bungee jumping and skydiving). The secular worldview offers oncoming death a cosmos that's dedicated to death. The fast lane is getting faster, and we'll flirt with death to escape the hopelessness the world offers.

In this dark universe, people turn to Eastern religions; Buddhists transcending themselves into Nirvana (the place of no wind where there is nothing) and good feelings without relationships or the boundaries that are created by the presences of others. Some world views promote healing of personhood while others destroy it because a Godless world will damage people. A health-promoting cosmos is friendly to personal beings and to personal relationships, with nurturing and significant qualities. Personal relationship is the key to emotional and mental health. Biblical religion is about relationships. The biblical theology worldview can stand up to secularism and paganism. Christians believe in it because it's true, not because it feels good.

We cannot define God, God defines Himself. We can define the word "God" in a language, we can understand it means "Creator of" and therefore sovereign over all that exists. If you are not "Creator" and sovereign, you are an idol pretending to be God.

The trinity is about relationships and community of three persons; Father, Son, and the Holy Spirit, three different persons in one God. The Father is the source of all being, eternal, perfectly formed and community of three persons. The voice of God is sovereign and has Spiritual authority for doing. It gives purpose for existence. There is communication between God and His creation called holy communion. We as Christians have access to the Holy of Holies and to the throne of grace. There is a flow of revelation and prayer between creation and God, a flow of energy between God and man for each other called "love." There is an open cosmos between God and us.

The Hand and Voice of God

With the Voice of God, God speaks to the world, commands the world, gives the world meaning, purpose and direction because God is the Creator and is responsible for its existence. He alone gives the world purpose; He and He alone gives the world existence. Our purpose for existence is so we can be moral and have meaning in life. In our relation to God, we have the Hand of God and the Voice of God that defines who God is as Creator and Sovereign. The Hand of God is our power of being. We stand on the Hand of God with our feet, trusting God with our whole weight of our being by letting go and letting God. This is our gift of grace given from God without charge.

The voice of God is the Authority for doing. Our security, personhood and being are guaranteed by God. God gives us freedom to accomplish what God requires of us. We don't have to do things (salvation by works) to secure ourselves, our being and personhood. "Who we are" without exception we are good, Paul tells us, "For every creature of God is good." (1 Timothy 4:4, KJV) and is to be received with thanksgiving. I can thank God for my being. "Being me" is something I don't need to justify because my existence and justification are given by the Hand and Voice of God.

God is like a battery; the Voice of God is the positive wire, which gives purpose for our existence and calls forth our being which is grounded in the Hand of God. The Hand and Voice of God are what connects us to Him and gives us purpose for our existence, to have relations with the created world and to light up the world. This connection we have gives power to our life. Our understanding of Creation, Fall and Salvation rests on our relationship with God. We trust God for our being and we obey Him in our doing.

Before the Fall, Adam and Eve trusted God for their being and were obedient in their doing. They received the power of life and submitted to His authority. They were promised a long life but if they rebel they would die. If we are not connected to Him, we will drift far from His Voice and His revelation and our lives will go into chaos. In order to hear God (revelation), we need to give up the world's independence and return to the Hand and Voice of God. People involved in the world have a hard time listening to God. It's difficult to open the door of trust and obey, but it can be done. When we disobey our purpose for existence, a separation from God occurs and we take the authority ourself to decide between right and wrong; good and evil. We step off the Hand of God into a world of doing it "our own way."

God has a story to tell. The Bible is about story and history, because the biblical cosmos is about persons in relationships.[10] We

---

[10] Macmurray, John. *Persons in Relation*. Atlantic Highlands, NJ: Humanities Internat. , 1991. Print.

are to make sense of God's story in a chaotic world. God is "human friendly." He is the Real Person, we can be real persons, in relationship with the Real Person. Only God can make us real.

The Perennial Philosophy

The Perennial Philosophy pops up where the biblical worldview is not accepted, when we walk off the Hand of God or refuse to obey His voice. The alternative to the biblical view is the Perennial Philosophy, which is the philosophy of the fallen world, a form of evolution.

"Apart from Me you can do nothing." (John 15:5). When we leave, there is no life anywhere apart from God, who is the Creator of all life. New Age talks about a mystical place called "Erewhon" (*nowhere* spelled backwards). This is the end of all things in the secular and pagan worldview. If the Bible is right, nowhere means "no place, nonexistence, a Godless state."

Death comes into a Godless world because the circle of the cosmos is not open to God, but closed. The cosmos is a "closed system" and "air tight." There is no communication from the cosmos to outside its circle because there is nothing outside with which to communicate. There is no "out there." The circle of the cosmos is closed. "And he will destroy in this mountain the face of the covering that is cast over all the people and the veil that is spread over all nations." (Isaiah 25:7). This is the death cloud. "Having their understanding darkened, being alienated from the life of God through the ignorance that is in them..." (Ephesians 4:18).

We move from graceful dependency and obedience to self-sufficiency, self-will, self-destruction, with a compulsion to do irrational things. We fall from grace into the world; from the blessings of heaven and its resources to a self-condemned place to do it on our own. The serpent cuts our relationship with God and we have to supply our own security of being and moral principles which don't exist in the fallen world, so we have to fake it.

Three Steps of The Fall

Romans 1:18 KJV, "For the wrath of God is revealed from heaven against all ungodliness and unrighteousness of men, who hold the truth in unrighteousness."

1.) Subversion of the truth, which leads to...
2.) Idolatry and dependency on the creation rather than the Creator, which in turn...
3.) Takes us to the inability to obey God.

All this leads to compulsive and self-destructive behavior. God will "give us up" to what we worship. If that's what you want, that is what you will get. We reap what we sow. The Fall is separation from God; the only one who can explain our existence and give it meaning. The Fall would have not been a fall if we were inherently autonomous. In the Fall there is no eternal life. Locking God out of our lives causes the death of a deep relationship. Secularism is the people taking charge of their own destiny and trying to rise above the power of death to delay it. Uroboros is a serpent in Greek Mythology that bites its own tail, creating a circular shape with its body. It represents a self-sustaining cosmos. This is what the serpent did to Adam and Eve; he cut their relationship with God.

The Stages in the Circle

Stage 1. The Great Mother (Greek mythology)
All things emerge out of the Great Mother, all theories of evolution use this pattern of eternal returns and cycles of nature. The Yin Yang (Chinese) is the center of all things, coincidence of opposites, the Womb of Life. Nirvana (Buddha), is the source of all being eternal, perfect, unformed, the antithesis of personhood.

Stage 2. Secularism
Life emerges out of animism (all rocks and plants have souls) and are outgrowing dependency on Great Mother into individuality; going over Uroboros and escaping death and taking charge of our own history by controlling resources.

Stage 3. Spiritualism

Human despairs of secularism and seeks solace by return to cycles of Great Mother and world-wide denying religions. Secularism collapses into (Neo) paganism of postmodernism and New Age no escape because Uroboros wins.

Stage 4. King of the Mountain

A sense of selfhood takes charge of man's history and meaning by control of resources."A pyramid of empires, a person at top with a crown. The pyramid has steps where other people are trying to take his crown in the competition for control and survival. It is the worldview of the Fall, closure of the cosmic circle of Hand and Voice of God. We feel no stability, existence feels accidental and as if the ground is sinking sand and we can't hear God's voice. God still holds us and speaks because we are alive, but we can't hear Him or discern His purpose for our life or have any moral principle because morals don't exist away from God. There is no Cosmic Intelligent Design.

Stage one begins at the center; Nirvana, the Womb of Life, and the Great Mother. The evolution of life in a world without God going to Erehwon (In New Age religion, it spells "nowhere" backwards.) Primitive tribes embraced Mother Nature and grew in personhood and individuality without an example or sense of a mature personhood. Their life is wrapped in the clan, custom and nature moving through the cycle of life into death and back to the womb.

As human consciousness becomes aware of its own individuality, it will value and experience itself as a somebody and will try to keep that self-hood. They themselves (the independent, autonomous decision-makers) begin building a pyramid to be King of the Mountain. Great empires are ruled by one king, but "uneasy lies the head that wears the crown."[11] The crown looks good among slaves, but there are other people trying to take his crown, or else he dies. Trying to run their own cosmos does not work, because death can prevail. There is no substantial meaning to all the

---

[11] *Henry The Fourth, Part 2 Act 3, scene 1, 31*

effort signifying nothing. In the end it does not produce the good life and returns to the comfortable womb of the Great Mother. The escape from Uroboros was only an illusion. The serpent relaxes his grip on his tail, stretches a bit, and takes us all in. There is no escape; "no exit."

In the Fall, God warned us that death will follow us (Isaiah 25:7). We made the wrong choice, and we ended up as victims of circumstances with no safe, secure place to rest our dependency. It is a world without purpose or moral principle. Moral doesn't exist without God, so we fake it. We fall into the world of emptiness and destruction. In the Fall, we descend into a downhill vortex into death. All people who live in the 20th century know it is true. Adam and Eve's decision and wrong choice to do it their way made us the victims, heirs, and perpetrators inclined to do what is evil, criminal or offensive.

In the closed cosmos of darkness, there is no person to whom you can say "I will trust you with the weight of my needs and my happiness." There is no one besides God; no one to whom you can say, "Your authority is worthy of obedience, I trust your leadership. I trust you and I am safe." In the dark cosmos, there is no eternal ground where we can stand and no eternal life. The hymn says, "All other ground is sinking sand,"[12] sinking nowhere, where relationships become a power struggle. The world becomes our God, with no secure foundation for our being or our doing.

Personal disintegration is the result in the pit of nothing and non-being. At birth, we leave the safety of our womb and go on a journey through enemy-held territory that has minefields. The only escape out of the pit of darkness is the Way of the Cross - Salvation and radical healing. The choice we make will determine if we are healed from our roots, or just covering the problem with a bandage. Since we live in a fallen world, there will be muddiness, a degree of not trusting or obeying because we live by grace.

---

[12] Mote, Edward "My Hope is Built on Nothing Less" *circa* 1834; first appeared in Mote's *Hymns of Praise*, 1836.

Gender - Depending on Your Worldview

The space between the Hand (mothering) of God and His voice (fathering) is all creation. This is where we live, move and have our being free to choose for or against God. Like a human parent, God holds us in His arms close, and we hear His heartbeat and see His face. This emotional space is seen between human parents and children. This space is needed to allow the child to make his own choices without too much pressure from the father's authority. The father can't be too far away where he is not available. The fathering side of God does not crowd us so we won't have freedom, nor is He too far where we can't feel His presence and direction. We are given a choice to obey or rebel. The choice to obey is our own choice and is not forced. This is the meaning of the two trees in the Garden of Eden.

The terrible twos and teen rebellion stages that seem negative are necessary for learning to say "yes" and "no" to our parents and God. Parents are to help their children learn to do that in becoming ourselves. Every child wants to "belong" to mother and father. Belonging is the child's security which he will experience in the space of love between both parents. The child does not want to be a slave or controlled by them. This will happen if the relationship between parents is unhealthy. If this happens, the child's maturation and healthy self-hood is cut at the knees, and they will experience this because the emotional space of love between both parents is not there.

When there is a relationship that's not healthy between parents, the child does not feel safe. He will be an unhealthy dependent, unhealthy independent, immature dependent or rebel. He will fail to mature and will experience belonging in a negative manner. In a good relationship between his parents, the child receives the gift of belonging. God created parents in His image and are to live in that image of health and holiness so that our children will feel safe, so when they mature healthily they can easily recognize God and meet Him.

In the closed circle cosmos (parents without God), there is no Hand of God and no moral stability guiding and sustaining them. The nurturing and guidance of the parents is limited because without God these qualities do not exist. A Godless culture breeds unhealthy citizens and children. This is seen in the decline of child raising in the last part of the 20th and early 21st century.

We can't define God, but we can define the word "God." God is Creator and Sovereign- the power to give existence, the power to create and the ability to give being is the Spiritual power. God gives us existence then tells us what that existence is for and why we are here. God gives His creation its reason for existence. That is His Spiritual Authority.

There are two defining characteristics of God; His Spiritual Power and His Spiritual Authority. All biblical theology flows from this definition of God; If you are not creator and sovereign then you are not God, you are an idol pretending to be God. Characteristics that define the image of God are He is personal, loving, omnipotent, omnipresent, sovereign, emotional and reasonable.

Our genders (male and female) made in the image of God is something in God of which men are an image. There is also something different in God of which women are an image. This is the logic of an image; it has to be two-way. If I am like God and made in His image, then something in God is also like me.

Men and women are made "in the image of God" embodying the spiritual power and spiritual authority of God, which are the ability to give existence and to give the purpose of our existence. Those are the mothering and fathering qualities in which image we are made male and female. We have them in a limited manner, but we have them.

It is not good that man be alone. Eve was made to minister to Adam's loneliness and to complement Adam's reason for being. Adam was not made to embody the life-giving side of God, he needed a "helper" to do that and to complement his own masculine nature as spiritual authority. He needed someone with the feminine gift of life-giving. The parents who are in God's image bring forth new life (children) who are raised up by the parents who have God's image so the children can be introduced to God and to recognize Him more easily and to receive Him.

The father's spiritual authority comes from the image of God. The father who is made in God's image embodies the Spiritual Authority of God to instill it into his children. The mother who is made in God's image receives the Power of being (to give life) from God to have children. The father assumes the role of manifesting Spiritual Authority he received being made in His image to instill this to his sons.

We are made in the image and likeness of God, male and female. Gender is based on the creation story of Genesis. Gender distinctions are "masculine and feminine." A male can have feminine attitudes or behavior. Fathers will be called to do some mothering. A female can have masculine attitudes and behaviors. Mothers will be called to do some fathering. Gender distinctions exist in God. Spiritual characteristics of gender (life-giving, Spiritual Power and Spiritual Authority) reside in God. Neither men nor women have this quality only given by God in order to bring life. God is not a physical person.

The existence in human persons of this dual character is commonly accepted. There is in men and women power of being and spiritual authority. The child will experience this dual relationship from the parents. In a healthy family, the child will receive the gift of mothering (giving and stability). The father will give the child moral and spiritual direction (the knowledge of their reason for being and also a mothering image). If the parent's image was bad, God takes the role of reparenting and will undo the damage done by the parents. A therapist will find ways to repair the damage done by parents and will sometimes try to take God's place in healing. That is something only God can do.

In God's plan, He wants you to have the experience of being a "child of God." To receive the experience of being mothered and fathered by God, resting the weight of dependency on the Hand of God and listening for direction from the Voice of God.

When our dependency is in the Hand of God, we don't depend on the creation, but on the Creator. When we listen to His voice and not other voices, nothing in the world will shake our stability.

In the battle of the sexes, the secular does not have the answer. The secular psychology states that "religion" brought conflict and war against morality. The morality of "religion" brings guilt that is destructive to the human nature. All this caused the "Death of God" movement. Death of the Father God, but not of "The Great Mother. The religion of God is dead, so the new religion of Mother Goddess takes its place by trying to justify immorality.

The Law of Love

Jesus was asked the meaning of the Law. Its the two Great Commandments, "To love God and to love one another." This is the Law of Love. This is the law of the prophets. The Hebrew scriptures contain the law and the creation story. The Law of Love is a commandment and is the purpose of our existence. The law of love is the highest law over creation. The law of love is the reason for our existence. Any law not in compliance with the law of love is not a law. Agape love is being dedicated to the welfare of another, doing things that help fulfill the life of that person. The law of love is the law of God for mankind.

Love is an obligation because its the will of God. It's a law; a commandment. Only in a biblical world can we become sons of God. Only in the biblical world can we be saved. Only in the biblical world can we be "born again." Only in the biblical world, the love between Father and Mother can create a space of love for her child. Only with a Biblical God can we have an inner marriage and receive inner healing.

The Health Problem

Half of the battle is won in defining the word "health." The Bible tells us what it is and how to pursue it. People don't know this, including doctors. Some don't agree that health and morality go together, that health has a moral sense and a moral element.

God requires the best of us and to be healthy. God is the absolute reality because He has the power to create all things, and He is Sovereign. In order to be healthy we must live in the presence of God. God defines "health" and tells us what is truly human.

Biblical health implies five things:
1. Health is not determined by culture, it is determined by God.
2. Physical and emotional health are built on spiritual health.
3. Health and sickness have two spiritual components; trust (security of being) and obedience (purpose for existence).
4. Our being (health) has to do with structure of our identity in His image.
5. Our being and stability are rooted in the "inner marriage," or "the experience of being created," (mothered and fathered) and directed by God Himself.

The biblical word is built on stability, moral direction, spiritual power and spiritual authority. These qualities are rooted in His image and in His image we are made, male and female. We are His creatures, not self-existing, eternal beings. Our health comes from our trust and obedience to God. The more parents (the first God-figures) lead children to trust and obey, the more secure will be the child's identity and boundaries.

Three fundamental questions for children:
1. Who can I trust with my security and needs that I cannot meet on my own?
2. What is the reason for my being, why am I here and who do I ask to find out?
3. Who can put my security and reason for being together so they don't conflict?

These are basic questions for physical and emotional health as well as for evangelism and spiritual health. Learning these questions will give us a foundation for intellectual, moral and spiritual maturity. Revival comes by returning our trust to the Hand of God and being obedient to His Voice. This is how emotional and physical health comes. Trust and obey is the theme of all scripture; its the way to abundant life. Jesus said, "If any man will come after me, let him deny himself, and take up his cross daily, and follow me. For whosoever will save his life shall lose it: but whosoever will lose his life for my sake, the same shall save it." (Luke 9:23-24 KJV). Following Jesus leads us to the Father in heaven so that all the blessing of the heavenly realm becomes ours beginning here on earth.

CHAPTER FOUR: THE FIVE DECISIONS TO BE WELL

In the deviated and deceiving world, we fall into emotional pits that are hard to get out of. There is no way out, the serpent just loosens its grip on us. The biggest problem is that we don't trust anyone to help us out, even God. There are five decisions we can make, no matter the circumstances, to go into the light of the truth. These decisions belong to us because we are alive. We are to have a proper understanding of how our human nature works. This is essential for spiritual growth because by digesting this key of truth, things will get better. Without this truth's decisions, we will be stuck in the darkness. Proper spiritual direction from a spiritual advisor is needed and must be aware if this key truths are pursued.

Without an assessment, it will be hard to progress. It is not true to say "If you believe hard enough, it will happen." Not with our own strength can we believe, will or choose salvation by works. It's by "grace through faith" that we believe, choose and will the truth. The truth we believe must be positive to get results. We must believe in order to get well. If the gospel is not truth, then our hope and healing are in vain. By making The Five Decisions To Be Well (to be whole, and be what we are created to be), we are participating in our own recreation and we become co-creators with God of our own personality by choosing to be made in His image.

We can build heaven with God by the choices we make or build hell all by ourselves. Being made in the image of God is the basic principle for child raising and maturing into adulthood. If I want to know who I really am, I must get to know God by making the five biblical decisions. When a child is in the dependent stage with their parents, it is when he is more vulnerable and can easily suffer damage that later gives him emotional and drug dependency. In this dependency relationship, the child is either nurtured and matured or he will experience damage. In healthy dependency relationships, we find cure to the damage done in an unhealthy relationship. Knowing the truth about the relationship and making good decisions leads to healing.

Now, healing doesn't just come by making good decisions, but if they are not made the bottled-up self will not come out. We won't come to the full knowledge of who we are as human beings.

We need our emotional life to come together with our spiritual life by allowing our key relationship with God to fix the lessor relationship. We can only be fully human by following Jesus and by allowing God to draw us into a relationship with Himself so He can redeem all of the damaging relationships. Apart from God there is no relationship that can redeem the past.

The key decision is to follow Christ, to come to the Father through Jesus, to be born again and to live in the power of the Holy Spirit. The decision to follow Christ is the key to our wholeness as human beings. Humanism is man putting himself at the center of the universe. It is man trying to be fully human, in his effort of self-creation, without the Creator.

We all have goals we follow. God also has goals and a purpose for us to follow in order to stay well. If we don't follow His goals, we won't function fully and sickness will come. Choosing God's goal for our lives is choosing to be well. The ultimate goal God offers is sonship and daughterhood in the family of God.

THE FIVE DECISIONS TO BE WELL

The Five Decisions are five basic decisions about life; five areas in life we all need to deal with. By nature we are goal-oriented and we choose a purpose for our lives and work toward that purpose. If we don't follow God's goals and purpose for our lives, we will live in contradiction against God and risk getting sick.

The Gospel of Jesus is true and it answers questions we ask as humans. The Bible does not just answer questions; its the best answer. The gospel is true because that's what it is; truth. It can reveal itself as truth. God can reveal Himself as God, the real God is the one who will show up as He promises. Just ask Elijah in I Kings 18.

In learning to live in a world that contradicts the truth, many people stop believing that there is truth and God out there. The unbeliever says "I believe abortion is wrong and I won't push my beliefs on those that believe abortion is okay. I won't tell the person he is wrong because he will feel bad." If truth is relative, then so is morality. The world's push away from truth in the name of personal freedom and "having it your way", the world goes into moral meaninglessness and moral chaos (or totalitarianism) which is the very enemy we sought to evade.

Students with chips on their shoulders have deep resentment against discipleship because they can't make their own decisions. They have a "victim" approach to life and feel they are continually being "told what to do." If you will not control your life, someone else will. If you don't control your behavior, that's reasonable and socially acceptable, then society will control your behavior.

Students can make five decisions that only they can make to be free persons:
    1. The faith decision.
    2. The dependency decision.
    3. The personal responsibility decision.
    4. The purpose life decision
    5. The community-love decision.

No one can prevent you from making these decisions because you are alive, a potential given by God. They bring one's personality into completion, fullness and strength. Without making these decisions, one's personality, sense of community and meaning in life falls into disorganization and disintegration. The feelings will not come out of their prison. Freedom apart from the five decisions is no freedom, it is a fake freedom a bondage in camouflage, a counterfeit, pseudo-freedom that follows good feelings and not relationships. Genuine freedom defines good relations and self-discipline to form them. These five decisions give us community. This is where God builds His Kingdom.

What is behind the phenomena of life? What is the real "I" doing in this bumpy world? Is there something or someone behind the world? I. Who am I? 2. Do I have eternal life? 3. Do I have meaning and purpose? 4. How do I fit?

Decision #1 - The Faith Decision

Christians have not been able to publicly explain why we believe the Bible or the Apostle's Creed. Christians have lost intellectual credibility because people have left pastors, going to psychiatrists and secular psychologists for emotional healing.

In the epistemology, the study of how we know what we know, we can get back our intellectual credibility. "And ye shall know the truth, and the truth will make you free." (John 8:32 KJV). Most of us know that last part and not the first part, or know who said it to whom. "If ye continue in my word, then are ye my disciples indeed." (John 8:31 KJV). If we let the implications sink in, it will set us free. The alternative to the truth is something less than the truth. Falsehood will not set us free, it will put us in bondage. We don't pursue the truth with all our hearts, mind and soul, we play with the truth. We don't believe the truth the whole truth and nothing but the truth will set us free. If we did we would be seeking it at all cost.

In the slippery slope of the Fall, Paul says in Rom. 1:18 they "suppress the truth" and hold back the knowledge of God. This takes us to idolatry where we are dependent on ourselves in disobedience to God.

Defining faith means being open to the truth, being vulnerable, to be touched by the truth intellectually, emotionally and spiritually by having a listening spirit and a teachable spirit. Truth is the only way to establish a successful relationship. Being open to the truth is a scary business. It is taking a risk of being wrong or unfriendly. What if it hurts when admitting the truth? We do not want to find out we are wrong, so we don't investigate the truth. We don't want the foundation of our faith dug up and exposed to the light of the day, it is too risky. What if we have been wrong all our lives?

We are masters at hiding the truth, we protect ourselves from danger, living in emotional and intellectually walled fortresses. We resist getting too close to God or letting God get too close to us. We resist God and our neighbor by not letting them get too close to our inner identity, fearing they will judge us if they find out who we are. The truth we fear is the truth about ourselves and those we are dependent on for our welfare, our inner self-acceptance and identity. The ability and the right to be ourselves "If they knew who I really am would they still love me?"

The Risk of Being Teachable

In the self-sufficient world, we are trying to live without God, we have a feeling that He is not there, and we are condemned to getting along without Him. The risk is that the truth may not be friendly, or there is no God in a meaningless world, a world that ends in a void; an abyss of nothingness. Do we have a God that is malevolent, wishing evil, capricious and changes abruptly without reason?

Our parents, who are God figures, could have told us not to expect anything in life and to build walls of defense to protect ourselves from evil, shoving our memories as children within us down into a bottle and putting a cork on it. The risk of opening the doors of our defenses is to expose ourselves to the truth. "Behold I knock at the door" says Jesus (Revelation 3:20). If the truth about life by nature is unfriendly, don't open the door, but if it is gracious and loving, open it.

The opposite of having a teachable spirit is having a hardened heart closed from being touched by the truth. "Your faith has made you whole." (Mark 10:52 KJV 2000). Our faith attitude is related to our being, we are spiritual sacramental beings whose spiritual center is God, He is in our spiritual throne room. We are designed by an Intelligent Designer to be open to the truth. We are designed to love one another as Jesus loves us. We are designed to be responsible for our behavior and to be under the authority of our Creator. When we don't follow this decisions we are open to attack and erosion. "Your faith has made you whole." This was not intellectual faith or correct belief to be healed. The woman with the issue of blood and the Roman centurion were pagans whom had no intellectual faith-training or upbringing because they were not Christians up to then. The faith Jesus was referring to was not knowledge, but a pre-condition of knowledge and an openness of spirit allowing the person to be touched by the truth.

The faith Abraham had was not intellectually strong. He was not a rabbi and would not have passed a rabbinical examination because he was pagan. Abraham didn't have a synagogue, rabbis, scripture, or anyone to confirm his voices from God from a biblical point of view. He had little knowledge about God. Abraham had openness of mind and an obedience of spirit which enabled him to hear God.

The fruit of the Revelation that Abraham received is in the Bible. Abraham was on a Spiritual journey into the unknown, led by a voice that offered something better. Abraham is the Father of Faith and established the biblical point of view that we can follow to check if it's the voice of God. "Faith" is the courage to risk the unknown based on what one knows. The sons of Abraham are the sons of promise; those who are open to reality knocking on their door. Biblical faith is being open to have an encounter with reality.

Come Let Us Reason

He is calling us to affirm our personhood when we have a relationship with Him. God stands in the arena of reality. Where else can He stand? God doesn't want you to believe in a blind fashion, He wants us to decide between the two trees of good and evil. "Choose this day whom we will serve." (Joshua 24:15). Elijah said "The God who answers by fire He is God." (1 Kings 18:24) Paul answers some opinions of the Corinthians about the resurrection. There is a need to know all the facts. We do our homework and we are open to the truth in areas of our experience and reason. We preach the resurrection because it is true. If it wasn't true, everything would be in vain. Let truth speak for itself, rather than our telling the truth what it must be.

The Sword of the Spirit is the Sword of truth used to slay the lies and deceits of the enemy. Truth (the Sword of the Spirit) is the only offensive weapon given to Christians and the only one needed in spiritual warfare because we are also given power to be witnesses.

If we are not committed to the truth everything else we build on that foundation will not be firm, and we will not be living by faith. We are saved by faith, saved by our full openness to reality. In our relationship with others, we are to be encouraging and exhorting one another into truth. However, Christians and non-Christians struggle to maintain their identity when there is a conflict and become defensive, refusing to allow certain issues to be discussed for fear of being shown wrong. To disallow open discussion feeds a defensive mentality that becomes a dark hiding place for sin and sick, neurotic spirituality. 1 John 1:15 says, "God is light and in Him is no darkness at all." To say that in God is not darkness is to say that God lives in open relation with the truth. John says, "Walking in the Light," is the decision to let truth speak to us.

Point of Freedom

The first fundamental point of freedom is the faith decision, the choice to seek truth and not personal comfort; to engage in self-discipline and be a truth-seeker. If this choice is not made it leads to bondage. To chose to be a truth-seeker for inner healing and peace, we need to leave the door open which can include pain and suffering in the remolding process for growth and stabilization. All Christians need to make an inventory that searches our motives, beliefs, and styles of life and compare them to the will of God. We must submit our personhood to the truth and be committed to a listening spirit. Knowing the truth is a roadway to reality. There is no other foundation for radical root healing. When all else fails, read the instructions of the Bible.

Decision #2 - The Dependency Decision

When we make the right decision to accept the truth, we can make the other decisions on what and where to rest the weight of our being (our dependency), and where we will be set free to be our real selves. Decision #1 is the faith decision. Decision #2 is to be alive and dependent on others. This is our human nature. We will always need things and others to exist. Dependency is a lack of self-sufficiency, depending on something or someone. By nature we don't admit our dependency and have a fear of being dependent because of past hurts that we become independent and autonomous.

Codependency addictions occur when our needs are met in unhealthy ways, leading to disruptive, addictive and idolatrous conditions. All addictions are idolatries depending on something less than God for things only God can supply. When we worship the creature rather than the Creator, we go into self-destructive behavior when we repress the truth (Rom. 1:18) then in turn we depend on ourselves (idolatry) and we don't obey God. The only healthy dependency relation is with God; all others are a bondage.

To introduce dependency and inner healing, we need to know:
1. What is the Spiritual life?
2. What are feelings?
3. From where do the deepest feelings come from?

What is the spiritual life? It is a life in the Holy Spirit. It is life in Christ and it is obedience to God. Applying it to all people universally, its what we do with our obedience and the issue of trusting and obeying.

Am I a creature? Is there a Hand of God upon which I stand, or am I autonomous? We do participate in our identity by the choices we make, but our internal identity comes from our God, by nature, by our family and culture. We don't supply the ability to be ourselves. There is no self-made man because our existence is a gift, for our existence we trust in God alone.

We are not born trusting; we are born dependent and mature into trust. We are to be like children, dependent and helpless, renouncing all illusion of self-sufficiency. Small children are not born trusting; nobody is. They trust what they see, they trust at a distance when hiding which is the meaning of trusting. Children don't understand the relationship, they understand being physically connected.

To understand our dependency, God stands above us. Our dependence comes in two forms. First, the Hand of God is where we stand and receive the power of being. This is the mothering side of God that sustains us, nurturing and giving us existence. Second is the Fathering side of God, the right to be ourselves, our sense of self-worth.

We have our needs met in relationships or objects, bank accounts, TV, family other things, something or someone outside ourselves upon which we rest our dependency, which becomes our "God." "Dependency" doesn't sound very spiritual, but it brings the spiritual life right down into the world of relationships, daily living and practical application. The center throne room is our ultimate dependency for something outside ourselves. Whatever is most important to us sits on the throne-the coach of the three-man soul team (body, soul and spirit). Healthy dependency is the only way we can securely tie together our spiritual and emotional lives. Dependency is tied to God, and the First Commandment "Thou shalt have no other gods" and the Fifth Commandment "Thou shalt honor thy father and thy mother" (Exodus 20: 3, 12).

In our infancy, our parents have our foremost important dependency relationship because they are as God to us. Violating our relationship with our parents is destructive because we are violating our relationship with God and reenacting the Fall of Adam and Eve's break with God. When you honor your parents, this lays the foundation for the redemptive process to be re-parented by God, the real parent.

To mature, we have to be open to the fundamental processes of mothering (trust, power of being) and fathering (obedience, authority for doing). Our parents made in the image of God male and female implant in us that image of God. The mother is to bring the child Godly mothering and the father is to bring the child Godly fathering. Mothering and Fathering are gifts from God through our parents. Some parents don't do a Godly job or put a Godly stamp on the child's soul, and as a result misshaping and distorting images of God.

Inner healing is the healing of this distortion by being drawn into the presence of the true Parent Being "born again," you are being re-parented from our broken family in the world into the family of God. We move from mother and father being God to their child, to God being both mother and father to the child when they are "born again."

By nature we don't like being called "dependent." Its an insult to our self-esteem and personal pride. This equates with being childish and immature. We prefer to be autonomous and independent. Secular psychology can't deal with basic issues of our dependency. The hand of God upon which we stand is our most basic dependency relation of all. Our loss of consciousness of that connection is the Fall, triggered by disobedience. We are "on our own", trying to be our own source of being, trying to "be me" by what we do rather than by what God is doing; it is salvation by works.

The soul has three parts; the intellect, will and the emotions (relations), like a three-man team. The faculty of the intellect it analyses the world giving us knowledge. The will is the choosing faculty. The emotional faculty is connected to relations. Every team must work together to win; the soul has to cooperate to be joyful. A team needs a coach to become a winner; someone outside of itself that can look at it, love it, teach it, criticize it, urge and exhort it on to perfection. The coach is what sits on the spiritual throne room. If God sits on the spiritual throne, it will teach the mind truth, teach the will righteousness, Godly obedience and God will integrate feelings, emotions and relationships.

When young, we don't know God, we get to know God through our parents. We perceive to know God through our dependency and obedience focused on our parents and things of the world. Our spiritual journey is to find God and ask Him to sit on the throne.

If your soul is not operating effectively and efficiently in good condition, ask who sits in my spiritual throne and fire him or it. If your mind is constantly telling you things opposed to your feelings and your will is caught in the middle, ask who sits in the spiritual throne room. I need to examine that person or thing and if it can do what is required of it for my health. If not, I need to fire that coach.

We as dependent beings, are dependent upon what is right at the core of our emotional health. For our emotional health and our emotional lives, the "God" question will always come up. We all have someone or something on the throne that will be God for us. It may not be the real God, but it will try to function as God for us.

What Are Feelings and Emotions?

In a good relationship I feel joy, I perceive myself in a good relationship. In a bad relationship, I feel hurt because I perceive myself in a damaging relationship. A feeling is a perception of a relationship. Feelings are relationship knowledge. With no relationships, no feelings would generate. I could have feelings of abandonment or loneliness, but not flourishing feelings that come with human life and community.

When bored we do not perceive relationships as rewarding or worthy of interest, so no life-inspiring feelings are developed (cosmic silence). Feelings that come from relationships are not intellectual perceptions. If I say, "I understand the meaning of your words" this is intellectual perception. If I say, "l was touched by what you said" that's a feeling response. Peter's first sermon brought the people to the awareness that their dependency was not in God. They had feelings, but they we not reaching out in mere feelings. They were reaching out of the perceived need to be right with God.

Emotions are distinct from feelings. An emotion is a reaction to a feeling. Anger is not a feeling, it's an emotion. It is a decision we make to a bad circumstance. We are responsible for our emotions different from our feelings. Feelings are a perception of a relationship. My feelings are a product of my input into the relationship. We produce our emotions. It is a chosen response to a situation that we felt. I produce more to the anger with which I respond to hurt than I do to the original hurt itself. I contribute to the hurt by my attitude toward life and circumstances around me.

Where Do Feelings Come From?

Our spiritual life is what we do with our dependency and authority relationships. If it is true that feelings are perceptions of relationships, that means that our feelings come out of our dependency and authority relationships and will emerge out of our spiritual life. Our feelings come from those relationships in which we have invested our dependencies, our relationship with our "God."

THE FIVE DECISIONS TO BE WELL

The only way out of the conclusion is to deny this, showing that we are self-sufficient beings in need of nothing outside of ourselves. The Eastern religions and philosophies which Westerners accept teach this. The Buddhist concept of Nirvana is to go into a state of nothingness and dressed up to look desirable.

In the world of personhood and community, we are dependent beings. For inner healing, if I want to change how I feel, I must not work on my feelings but my relationships. My dependency is on my relationships not my feelings. To change my deepest feelings, I look at those deepest dependency and authority relationships of my life.

The separation of feelings from relationships and closure of the circle about oneself is the Fall. It cuts right at the meaning of the personal cosmos reducing it to impersonalism. Jesus did not give philosophical theories about God. He presented the person of God; He introduced God to us personally. If we get the personhood right, we can get theology right.

Who or what is on the throne of your spiritual center? Can it carry the weight of your being? Is it willing and able to support and sustain you in all your needs? Can it be the "coach" of your soul? Can it teach your mind truth, your will justice and righteousness? Can it integrate your feelings and relationships? If not, is there anything else in the universe more capable or more willing?

To make fundamental changes, we wonder why little happens; we want quick fixes and easy answers so we tinker with our feelings through drugs, alcohol, sex, money and power. We are creating a pseudo-relationship (counterfeit, false), a fake substitute for relation, trying to produce the fruit of relationships (good feelings) without personal responsibility.

The First Decision is to seek truth for healing and health. The Second Decision is the stability decision to rest our dependency on the rock (ground) that will securely sustain us. "I trust you fully and completely with my whole being, my welfare, and my happiness and I know I will be perfectly safe." There is no god or goddess in the closed circle of a Godless cosmos that we can trust fully. We must choose that being upon whose power alone we trust. We can stand on the Hand of God, who is the ground of our being. We must choose to rely on God as sustainer and nurturer, the mothering side of God.

Christians are those who have chosen Jesus, the Son of the living God, as the path to the ultimate dependency relationship. Christians are those who take Jesus' words in their proper context. "If you continue in my words, you are truly my disciples and you will know the truth and the truth will make you free." John 8:31 is a conditional statement. "If you want to find the truth follow me. I will show you exactly where it is and it will set you free."

Responding To The World

Every human being is looking for a safe haven, a place to rest his dependency that can only be found in the gracious nature of God. If Christians retain their intellectual and moral credibility they will have a good testimony, a genuine provision for the universal dependency need. In the Christian, Jesus is on the throne of the spiritual center, through whom we have access to the Father and to life in the power of the Spirit of God rather than life in our human strength. This dependency decision corresponds to the greatest commandment, Matthew 22:37 "You shall love the Lord your God with all your heart and all your soul and all your mind." In the deepest level of my being, I allow God to uproot all those dependencies that get in the way of His being our true and only dependency.

Matthew 7:13, "The narrow gate is wide and easy that lead to destruction and many enter it. The narrow gate is hard that leads to life and few find it."

The decision to be well is the decision to rest our dependency in God and to risk whatever it takes to get there. That is the journey of spiritual growth and healing. Dependence in the world ends in the same place. In mutual dependencies we expect support from each other, complete for love, affection and respect. We have to earn our way through life and the right to be ourselves. We get trapped in a system that cannot stop being manipulative, selfish, malicious and destructive. We become cynical and sarcastic about human relationships. There does not seem to be any secure place I can rest my need for intimacy. "Intimacy without God is cannibalism" we eat each other up. The risk of investigating our dependency down to its roots is plunging to the very foundation of our being to see if it's solid. Only a secure relation with God will make our dependency something we can accept and rejoice in. Without God we would despise, hate, avoid and deny our dependency in Him. This is what makes us vulnerable to the frustrations and defeats of this world and then death comes.

The risks of Decision #1 The Faith Decision and Decision #2 The Stability Decision are worthwhile only if the Great Unknown is Friendly Unknown. Our fallen imagination is programmed to picture a very unfriendly unknown. Jesus proved this different when he said, "Come let us reason." The decision to be open to the truth and to put my dependency on Christ, my area of freedom increases. I am in touch with a power that sets me free to be who I am because I am unconditionally created and accepted for who I am. To accept Jesus as Savior is to trust God for sustaining, nurturing power, and the ability to be myself. That is the mothering side of life. I have put myself in His hands, and He accepts responsibility for my being.

Point of Freedom: Understanding The Dynamics of Dependency

The biblical paradox makes sense that "In my weakness is the strength of God made known" (2 Corinthians 12:9). Only by admitting my weakness, my inherent dependency, can I allow myself to become a dependent of God. In abandoning myself to God I find myself enduring. The little baby in me, my weakest part, becomes the channel of Godly strength. My childhood in God is the foundation of my adulthood in the world.

I choose where I will rest my dependency for my safety and security and for my ability to be myself. When Christians say they have come into relation with God, who can supply "forgiveness, wholeness, health, well-being and abundant life," which is the biblical meaning of salvation, the healing and resolution of our feelings and emotions part are what salvation means. God alone can sustain the burden of our dependency needs. Healing and freedom do not come from tough circumstances, or "toughing it out," though we may be required to go through it. Healing comes by learning to let go so God can supply the needs for nurturing and direction. There is a part of us that fears being loved because we fear being let down again. As long as we are dependent on things short of God, those things will let us down. We fear letting go for it seems to make us soft rather than tough it out. But the unconditional love of God does not lead to weakness, it leads to strength that undo the worldly. Only as we become children (dependent, obedient bearing the image of the parent) in God we can be adults (independent, free, a somebody). In the world, the most-stable thing in all existence is the image of God. It will never change. That means the second most stable thing in all of existence is a person fully made in that image.

Standing on the Hand of God and obeying His voice secures the being and identity of any person against the slings and arrows of the enemy. Nothing can pull the rug out from under Him. He will always be able to be himself fully in the presence of any person anytime. Over against all the dependency choices of the world, the freedom given by Jesus is the alternative to the world. Jesus is not dependent on the world to be Himself and can sustain the rest of us who are dependent on Him. The world cannot offer that.

If the biblical answer is not correct, then there is no answer to the deepest needs of the human heart. We just have to make the best of a bad situation and are forced into the resources of the world itself that are inadequate; becoming self-sufficient and independent. If we make this decision about whether to be transparent or not, what you see is what you get.

Decision #3 - The Personal Responsibility Decision

Who is responsible for what? The first decision is to seek the truth, and the second is to rest our dependency in God. The biblical answer for our dependency is God. If the biblical answer is true, all other answers are idolatry. We use the freedom that we received through our secured dependency by accepting full responsibility for our behavior, attitudes and reactions. Responsibility comes in two ways; personal responsibility and moral responsibility. Personal responsibility means I did something and acknowledge that I am personally responsible for it. I experience myself as responsible.

You can gain independence from your mother so that you are not an appendage (attached) to her. The "terrible twos" are where we learn to say "yes and no" appropriately. If I take responsibility for my actions, reactions, thoughts and behaviors, my "yes" will mean "yes" and my "no" will really mean "no." Once I make The Personal Responsibility Decision, I can no longer say, "You made me angry!" I can say, "You caused me pain," but it was myself that got angry and caused damage as a response to the hurt and pain. I must accept responsibility for my anger. Pain and loneliness can be caused by others but only circumstantially. It is temporary; they come and go. But the damage we cause comes along with us. God will help us grow beyond the unhappy circumstances if we remain in the relationship. Our self-caused damage prevents us from growing past the circumstances because the walls of unconfessed sin inhibit God from His freeing and healing work in us. Understanding this principle can prevent pain and false guilt from coming upon us.

In a marriage, we shift blame where it does not belong or receive it when we are not guilty. We are "made to feel guilty" because of the emotional reaction of another person. We feel guilty for their pouting, twisting of the lip, the cold shoulder and temper tantrum as if we have caused it. We are responsible for our behavior, not theirs. We could have done something to inspire and encourage their behavior, but we did not cause it. We may be responsible for some of the hurt they feel but not for their reaction to the hurt. The other person has to stand trial for his behavior. We have our own trail to stand. Adam and Eve were the first to practice scapegoating, looking for someone to blame. The serpent is responsible for trying to seduce Eve into temptation; Eve is responsible for listening to the serpent and giving Adam the forbidden fruit. Adam is responsible for eating it. We have to bear our responsibility.

Taking responsibility for my behavior is different from accepting responsibility for myself. God is responsible for my being; my being is God's doing. I am responsible for my doing, not for my being. We are responsible for our own doing. This distinction may seem pedantic and arbitrary but it is biblical. I am not responsible for my being because I do not cause my being, God is. But I do cause my own behavior. I am responsible for what I cause, not for what God causes. Who I am is God's gift to me and to others, given unconditionally. What I do is my gift to God and to others. I receive God's gift to me and accept myself from God and put my dependency on Him. I have to be open and honest in my relationships about my use of that gift of selfhood.

The Personal Responsibility Decision is exercising our freedom in a responsible way. Selfhood develops only as we take responsibility for our behavior, attitudes and reactions. Decision-making is part of selfhood, and responsible decision making is the only way to maturity as persons. We form purposes for our lives that form our personal boundaries. The child in a dependency stage has less freedom to take responsibility for his behavior. He is still in the process of The Five Decisions that the child cooperates (or not) with God to make him a free and rational person. We cannot be fully adults without God. The parent is in the place of God and has much influence in the dependency stage of a child. The child has a deep dependency at a time when he can't make adult decisions. The child is not responsible for his behavior or reaction, in the same way, as an adult. As an adult, I am responsible for dealing with past inner memories and not staying in my childish or sinful behavior. The question is not what caused the damage, but what my behavior could have been or can be (more responsible, compassionate, righteous and just).

I am as an adult responsible for bringing the Gospel to that child in me and for bringing an attitude of obedience to God and love of my neighbor, even if my neighbor is the father who abused me as a child. We take Godly authority over our past life however painful or damaged it may have been. Once I take responsibility for my behavior, attitudes and reactions, I will have a new measure of freedom. Every time I say, "You made me angry," I have given away my freedom and have made myself a yo-yo on someone else's string. I am a sailor in the sea of self-pity and blaming the circumstances for my behavior, attitude and reaction on someone else. This is called the "victim syndrome." When I say, "What I did was my fault," I take back my freedom and begin to be restored to self-control. I can feel like a surfer who rises up on a wave or a sailor who has caught the wind in his sails. It is not a false effort to be free, or to appear to be righteous when we are not giving away our freedom that we seek.

By taking responsibility for my behavior, attitude and reactions, I am serving notice that you may hurt me and cause me pain and frustration and influence me and how I feel, but you cannot control my behavior or my reaction to being hurt. Recognizing this principle would set us free from guilt and resentment. The real nature of responsibility, guilt, repentance and forgiveness is by knowing who is responsible for what. Having put our being in Jesus' hands, we focus our repentance on the area of our doing, not the area of our being.

Responding To The World

Our parents are in the place of God for us as infants and point us in the direction of God. When rules of God are followed they yield results. Only when we are dependent of God are we free from the temptations of the world, the flesh and the devil, to compromise our integrity.

Boundaries for Freedom - The Discovery of Freedom

In the "terrible two's" and the "teen-rebellion" we can say "yes" or "no" that we are somebodies in our own right. We discover a little kingdom, a small domain called "mine." We discover the two trees in the Garden of Eden, one leading to life and the other leading to death; the fork at the road. At about eight years old we experience the freedom to "think for ourselves" to spar with dad about the meaning of "life" leading to growing teen independence.

Boundaries can keep us out or keep us in; they can keep others out or lock them in. They can be freeing or put us in bondage; decision-making requires boundaries. The making of a decision is a declaration of selfhood and freedom. It is my decision. God has bestowed upon us that characteristic of Himself, freedom, which is decision-making. This creates boundary lines that divide between "me" and "you" which creates community. We discover ourselves as decision-makers and different from others because we are beginning to make-decisions "over and against" parents and others. The against is not antagonistic. The way is to navigate our differences and antagonisms into harmony of the Kingdom and the community. Freedom does not come because we choose; our human nature is meant to be free, but can be broken by our choices. We must follow the structure of freedom to be free, navigating the structure of freedom by following The Five Decisions.

We think that the law and grace are opposites; grace is friendly and the law is tough on us. Grace has its own discipline. It forms in us the capacity for freedom. The law is an act of grace. These three decisions are the discipline of grace, which puts ground under me to handle the fourth decision; the discipline of law. Without the Decision #1 - The Faith Decision, Decision #2 - The Stability Decision, and Decision #3 - The Freedom decision, the fourth decision, The Discipline of the Law, cannot be made. I will not survive it with my freedom. The Law no matter how loving, will threaten and oppress my security and my boundaries will be unsecured.

God is building strong free persons who can respond to His call. With God, the law and grace go together providing strong, capable, sturdy and free sons and daughters of God. Making this decision for our own stability of freedom and integrity will prepare us for the next decision to "reason together" with God about the meaning and direction of life and whether we want to sign on to a covenant with Him to be baptized.

Decision #4 - The Morality Decision (Morality Law and Purpose for Life)

For the child, "important" means "what father and mother require." The unimportant is "what they let me choose." Parents are in a God-role. The child understands himself as "coming from their parents," that they are his source and from where his existence started and he is responsible to them. Moral authority under God is the same. It is our spiritual journey with our mother and father to a place where we recognize God as our mother and father, and we are nurtured and governed by God as the voice of sovereignty. The Voice of God is our true conscience. The Voice of God joins the Hand of God and creates a space between mothering and fathering which in the child dwells. It is a deep faith-dependency-obedience relationship governing all life.

Spiritual Authority complements spiritual power; fathering complements mothering. Moral Authority is the ability to decide the reason for existence, our reason for having life at all. God, the Creator, is able to decide the reason for existence for all things and all persons because He is the Creator and giver of them. If there is a Creator, moral obligation is about determining why He created us and then pursuing that purpose. The life decision is the most basic of all moral decisions. The Authority of God is directed at the intentions and doing of all creation symbolized in humans by our voices and our hands.

We affect the world by our speech and our activities. My moral obligation is to choose to conform my purposes in life with His purposes for my life. Giving our life to God does not mean that

I have no will or choices, I freely choose to conform my choosing to His. Moral responsibility is beyond the personal responsibility because I now decide to be responsible to a higher authority than myself. It is one thing to admit that I did something and its another thing to be accountable before some other person for my behavior. Full responsibility requires both personal (#3) and moral responsibility (#4). In the dependency decision (#2) I seek to rest my dependency on the ground that's dependable, the Hand of God. In the reason for life, or the moral responsibility decision, I seek the highest authority and place myself under that authority, the will of God; under Abba the heavenly Father "He who decides." God can and God alone can decide my purpose for my existence. I place myself under the eternal purpose for my life.

In our fallen state, we tend to impose or force this decision upon ourselves or have it imposed on us before the three previous decisions have matured. In the moral responsibility decision, I invest my ultimate loyalty (faith) with stability, because the first three decisions have prepared me to make trustworthy and reliable decisions. The first three decisions prepared my personal boundaries of my personal kingdom, my selfhood. Our crowns we will cast down around the glassy sea, in offering to God.

Salvation requires that our doing flows out of our being (grace). Our being does not flow out of our doing; this is salvation by works. We are ourselves by what God is doing in us and not by what we are doing. The gift of our being is by grace, mediated through our mothers and purpose. Direction is meditated by our fathers. Fathering affirms the mothering gift and adds authority of purpose for existence, discipline meaning and moral order. To be created does not make me into the fulness of personhood. I am created in the image of God, but I am also being created in His image. That creating of me is something I participate in through my decisions. The ever-present fork in the road, significant by the two trees in the Garden of Eden.

When I ask Jesus to be my Savior, I give Him responsibility for my being and have a relationship of the deepest kind of trust

(Decision #2 - Dependency). When I ask Jesus to be my Lord, I put my doing under His authority and move into a relationship of the deepest obedience (decision #4 morality). I then ascend with Jesus in my heart and mind to the heavenly throne; I become a child by obedience to the heavenly Father. To accept Jesus as Lord is to accept Him as the one who leads me to the Father. The Father gives me my goals, affirms my worth as a person, my right to be myself and calls me into an adventure of spiritual growth and maturity. In John 4:34 Jesus said, "My food is to do the will of Him, who sent me and to accomplish His work." What brings us into fullness and maturity as sons and daughters is our obedience to the Father. A spirit of disobedience or rebellion or willful independence will abort our growth as mature, free-standing adults and return to the Fall. As Jesus leads us to the Father, we hear His voice, a word of command. God's purpose for our existence is to align our wills freely with His will. Before the Father, we stand responsible in a final and ultimate way.

Responding to the World, Moral Order - Trusting the Hand of God

Obeying the Voice of God comes from making Decision #2 - The Dependency Decision, and Decision #4 - The Morality Decision only if these decisions are rooted in Decision #1 - The Faith Decision. The first decision is about myself seeking truth for my benefit. Decision #3 is about speaking the truth in relationship and sharing truth for unity and community. Decision #4 says if there is no God then I am not responsible to anybody and have no moral responsibility at all. This gives Christians a powerful challenge to the world of a closed circle. Can our view provide our reason for existence?

Point of Freedom

I know what true righteousness is and what true holiness is, and I am set free to pursue righteousness and holiness. Putting myself under obedience to the Father, I become a child of God. To be an adult in the world, I must be a child in God. One who is a child of God and dependent on God, in the world I must be a child in God. One who is a child of God and dependent on obedience to the world can never be fully an adult in the world. I will be an adult-child of the world. I can never really grow up. As a child of God, I can now be in the world but not be of it, not dependent or obedient to the world. I can be fully in the world engaged in relationships. Those who are of the world will always be defensive toward relationships and are not really in the world, just of it. This is what Jesus meant when He said the meek would inherit the earth, those who are dependent on and obedient to God will be able to engage fully and openly in the world of relationships. By making these decisions, I will be prepared to follow the two highest laws in the cosmos, the two Great Commandments. I will be grounded in the grace and the law of God to love God and my neighbor.

Decision #5 - The Faith, Love, and Hope Decision (The High Ground of the Kingdom Plateau)

It is a difficult climb up through the first four decisions to the Kingdom Plateau of faith, love and hope. There are five decisions to go up to the Kingdom Plateau. Decision #1 - Faith (reality contact), Decision #2 - Dependency (power of being), Decision #3 - Personal Responsibility (integrity), and Decision #4 - Moral Responsibility (reason for existence). These four decision will allow you to make Decision #5 - Faith, Love and Hope the Kingdom Plateau.

Faith, love and hope are the three that endure; we reach a place of stability, the peace that passes understanding. In Decision #4, I choose to obey God, but I have not chosen specifically. In Decision #5, I choose concretely, beginning with the highest command. I can look around for ways to apply that. The first four decisions are needed to enter the faith, love and hope plateau. I cannot be an effective lover of God or of souls except by the other decisions. The degree of my relationship with Decision #5 will complete and sanctify us to enter the Kingdom plateau.

THE FIVE DECISIONS TO BE WELL

Love is acting for another's welfare and not counting the cost. The first four decisions gave us a practical definition of love being truthful, stable, honest and righteous in relation to another being and helping them enter into the fullness of that life which is the Kingdom. The fifth decision is to live fully in the life of God in the world of relationships in the "real" world. I renounce my commitment to "feeling good" at the expense of a relationship. I am resting my desire and expectation for good feeling on the relationship. I am putting my comfort at risk in a relationship. "My good feelings concerning you will depend on how you freely love me, not on how I can manipulate or control you."

Faith is how I live out of the stability of my past; love is how I live in present relationships and hope is how I aim into the future based on my faith and love. Faith is the conservative side preserving the lessons of life learned out of past experience. Hope is the liberal side looking ahead to new life not yet discovered. Hope is looking ahead to new life, new freedom and new truth.

When a non-Christian says "Well, I hope so," is not the Christian hope based on past and present reality contact. Absolute truth with God is faith in the trustworthiness of God. Love is how in the present I relate to persons. The present is where past-faith and future-hope connect. Love is that by which they are energized. The triad of faith-love-hope stands on the four previous decisions, the product of growth into maturity. We are told to be in the world, but not of it. We live in light and transparency, but our source is to be outside the world. Love is a decision to act out life fully in the world, but not to be of it. To be a sacrament of the life of God is to be an outward, visible sign of the inward spiritual love of God.

Being of God, I can invest myself safely and freely in the world. The self-designed worldly person cannot do that. I make the passion of the Messiah my passion. The law of love becomes the supreme law of my relationships with the community of creation. It becomes the definition of my purpose for existence. Not letting the sins of the world turn me into less than a loving person. If my wife does not meet my needs, I will love her nevertheless. If my children don't obey me, I will still love them. If I don't get a raise, I will love my boss anyway. Loving the world involves all the toughness of spiritual and moral authority and of speaking the hard truth. It is a decision to work, pray, and give for the welfare of those around me regardless of behavior, attitude or reaction on their part. To do whatever I can not to pamper them but to have an opportunity to come freely into the Family of God. My loving them freely is a response to God and the nature of His Kingdom only secondarily to my neighbor. Any other way of doing it will not work, it will be less than loving to my neighbor. My neighbor might prefer to be pampered and "have his way" rather than have the Kingdom of God opened up to him. But I am to obey God with the moral decision (#4) in the matter, nevertheless.

The fifth decision rests on the maturing power of the previous decisions to bring me into my selfhood. The moral decision (#4) puts this emerging selfhood at the disposal of God and His people. The self emerges from making the five decisions and then is released into the Cross, the stage of spiritual maturity where I am able to "get out of the way" and myself becomes, not a block, but a window to God. My selfhood can become "unconscious", hid in Christ, something I know I can rely on. Being fully me is to entrust my being to God, my doing and my obedience. The self that is dependent on worldly circumstances has died so the self dependent on God can live. I can forget myself and can reach out and focus beyond myself with agape love to the needs of the world around me. I become selfless. The self does not disappear or get annihilated, but it's not the focus of my attention. It is resting safely in the Hand of God. This selflessness is not that taught by Eastern philosophies and religions which lead to the annihilation of self, an impersonal religion. The Bible alone of all scripture and philosophies tells us that the community, family and agape love are the purpose and meaning of life. God is calling us to live a radical kind of life fully and totally in relationship in the real world, no hiding, no defense mechanism, with nothing less than the truth. Like Adam and Eve naked and unashamed, and John's "walking in the light." It is the opposite of the mediocre and inferior half-life many Christians live. Live in a radical Freedom to be totally myself and to share that self to lay that self down for the welfare of others knowing that will be sustained and guided by the Hand and Voice of God.

Responding To The World - The Higher Ground

Secular people have persuaded the world that they stand on the intellectual and moral high ground and that the spiritual high ground is irrelevant to the good life. Christians have lost their testimony in the public arena and to their shame, have little that is persuasive. God created, owns and stands on a higher intellectual, moral and spiritual ground, and He is inviting all creatures to stand there with Him. That high ground is the Kingdom; it is a reality. When we leave God, when we Fall, we lose contact with reality, and it erodes not only with God, but we lose first moral and spiritual high ground. We pretend to hold intellectual ground, but truth and commitment to truth do not long survive the loss of moral security in God.

We compromise truth for personal position and pleasure. This leads to pathological and diseased societies and citizens. For healing, we need to identify where the high ground is and how to get there. This is what God does; He shows us to get back in touch with reality, the Kingdom Plateau, the only substantial High Ground. The High Ground will either be a version of the Tower of Babel or following Jesus to the Father. The Five Decisions will light up the road to the High Ground of Faith, Love and Hope.

What is Love?

The world does not know what love is. They think it's to lust after or to like a lot. We say, "I love ice-cream" or when we end a conversation we say, "Love ya." Love means "I will lay my life down for you." Liking things or persons is a good thing, it is a bad thing to mistake it for love. We are commanded to love, not like one another. Biblical love is to dedicate my resources, time and talent to your welfare. I may or may not like you. Liking a lot indicates lust, but if I love you, I will never lust after you. Love and lust are contradictories.

The world can't maintain a proper relationship between feelings and relationships because of its defensiveness and distancing from relationship. In the world a person, in order to feel good, will compromise in a relationship. When we like someone we are tempted to control them to keep them satisfying our needs, manipulate their admiration and respect because that makes us feel good. We don't love them we need them. We are dependent upon them, we are their children and are not in an adult relationship. Most marriages are built on a foundation of needing and liking, not loving.

The Christian can explain love, that it is grounded by faith which is openness to the truth and that it points forward in hope to the future. Godly love is rooted in the most unchangeable thing in existence, the image of God, in which we are made male and female, fathering and mothering.

Through The Five Decisions, God builds us into strong, stable adults in the world by making us children in Him. We go up the mountain of spiritual growth to Kingdom Plateau, the place where Kingdom relationships take place, where faith, love and hope take place.

Point of Freedom

Westerners are ignorant about love and freedom. So-called "liberal" (secular) Democracy, the pinnacle of freedom. The freedom to do as we like, the freedom offered by the serpent, to be god-like. This is the biblical definition of sin, inventing one's own reason for existence, rejecting the Sovereignty of God, each doing what is right in their own eyes. God gives us freedom to make The Five Decisions. Into spiritual maturity, we are freed to become truth-seekers, to be dependent, real, open and honest selves and seek righteousness, our reason for being and to be lovers of souls. God's freedom leads to wholeness of our creature-hood; the world cannot offer this freedom, and there is a compulsive power struggle comprised to stamp out such freedom. We have the ability to do it without God, but we lose our moral freedom. God's commandments to love God and neighbor are the two highest laws of the cosmos. The law of love is the Ultimate Constitution for the cosmos. God sent the Hebrews to the back side of the desert to see if they would obey His commandments. He also sends us into a Spiritual Journey for the same reason. A dangerous Journey from the mother's womb into life to choose whether to build heaven with Him or hell all by ourselves. We have the ability to go to Hell, but we do not have the right. Our right is the same as our obligation to build heaven with Him and each other. God's freedom requires the discipline of grace, the discipline of the five Decisions. At every Decision we are trained and set free by the grace of God.

The freedom of Christians comes from the grace and law of God. All other freedom is rebellion and a delusion (falsehood) that leads to death of the forbidden tree. Only God can set us free, not the world, the flesh, nor the devil. The message of freedom is to be truth-seekers, seekers after righteousness and lovers of souls in order to be children of God. This is a message Christians must proclaim to the world. It is a freedom which the world, the flesh and the devil will work to kill.

The Five Decisions form the structure of freedom for all created beings. The foundation of Christian discipleship and healing is having God's freedom who gives us a healthy notion of selfhood and freedom. These truths are the foundation for Christian healing or discipleship ministry. The five Decisions together compromise the discipline of grace, faith, love and hope.

Putting The Five Decisions to Work

It is not possible to deal with emotional illness without dealing with the spiritual person. Other ways will alleviate the pain and give joy, but healing the biblical way is permanent. We need to ask "Who or what is God in my life?" The key decision to being well to be whole is the decision to follow Jesus as Lord and Savior to be holy. Anything less than this will leave some rooted problem unresolved.

CHAPTER FIVE: THE GROWTH OF PERSONAL FREEDOM

Each decision gives a new point of freedom and a deeper affirmation of our identity. With The Five Decisions we mature into adulthood. If any level is missing or defective, our personhood is left inadequate and incomplete. Each decision adds to our "courage to be." In each decision, we participate with God in our creation. They are decisions not even God can make for us. He is calling us into decisions in which we freely choose to participate. In the first decision, we are truth seekers. We make a commitment; we want to know more, we are curious, which is part of having a teachable spirit of faith. As we mature, truth-seeking stabilizes the ground of our lives in truth. This is The Decision of Truth. The second decision, we discover that the truth is a "Who" not a "What" and discover Who "the truth" is, as children dependent of the Truth, who is our personal Creator God. We discover what it means to be mothered by God. Even when we leave the family nest we are still being mothered by a heavenly Parent. The answer to "Who am I" is really "Whose am I." We discover God as the Ground of our being and the true lover of our souls.

The nature of the mothering side of God gives us stability. We are adults with God; we can say yes, and we can say no with a trust-worthy word, able to acknowledge our behavior and stand with integrity in a relationship. We discover ourself as speakers and doers.

In The Fourth Decision, we discover ourselves as sons and daughters of the Highest Authority in the universe. We are morally responsible before God; we have a purpose to life; our being. We have a place in the Father's plan and heart. In The Fifth Decision, we become obedient lovers and servants of God. God is the lover of our souls, and we also become lovers of souls by participating. This forms our identity in Christ made in the image of God. This is the decision of perfection, Matthew 5:48, "Be ye perfect." We become completed and perfected in God. We are fully in the world but not of it. The meek will inherit the earth, not the "worldly." Every level of our freedom is increasing.

Discipline is necessary for freedom; it is not an enemy. It is the ability to choose rationally, realistically and freely between the two trees; The Tree of the Knowledge of good and evil or rebellion and the Tree of Life, trust and obedience, the fork in the road. It requires the incorporation of all five decisions. We are being created as intelligent designers by the intelligent Designer. The process begins with the decision for truth and is completed by the decision for love. Love keeps the prior decisions from unraveling and locks them in. It is the willingness to suffer for the sake of the relationship rather than betray relationship for good feelings. This is a living process, designed and overseen by a loving Father.

Early sins and errors are redeemable; anything can be changed. Only as we make the truth the whole truth and nothing but the truth our first agenda will our spiritual life grow, mature and become stable. Persons with this kind of freedom become invulnerable to the disasters of the world.

Five Levels of Repentance

Truth

Christian therapy contains an examination of motives, behavior and also a spiritual inventory. When we want something less than the truth because of a hardened heart, we have to repent. We have to develop teachable spirits intellectually and emotionally. A hardened heart will twist and manipulate the truth and will become unaware of what is happening. The more we twist the truth, the more we lose the ability to distinguish between true and false.

Dependency

Dependency is the second decision; it is creating stability. Being open to the truth is the first decision but has no concrete foundation. Its only desire is to know "what is," that truth is a person. Commitment to the truth is not to know what truth is, it is only the beginning. Concrete commitment begins with decision two, dependency. We move into the most concrete and personal of decisions. A concrete material increase is our freedom and ability.

Ultimate Truth is a person; people need the truth to govern their affairs properly. We must repent of our obsession with independence and spiritual autonomy and rebellion against dependency on God and against our legitimate human dependencies.

We are dependent beings, our quest for independence and autonomy without God will lead us into idolatry. We are dependent beings and will always be dependent on others. If we refuse God, we become dependent on wrong, inadequate things in the closed circle of the fallen world. The dependency decision is a personal decision, and object of my dependency decision is God, who is a person.

Life-Truth is a personal and concrete commitment. Being open to more truth and changes in one's perception of the truth as the truth further explains itself and clears our blind spots, biases, misconceptions, misinformation and rebellion. The decision to rest one's dependency somewhere is the primal (chief) "God" decision. It is a concrete and personal decision where the process of growth, individuation and loving relationships must take place. "For in Him we live and move and have our being." (Acts 17:28). We must repent of trying to live anywhere else.

Personal Responsibility

We must repent of subverting (corrupting) our maturation by not taking responsibility for our behavior, attitudes and reactions. Blaming and condemning others is an inadequate, sinful and forbidden way to establish our selfhood. "Judge not, that you be not judged." (Matthew 7:1). The personal responsibility begins during the "terrible twos" when we are first experiencing our independence from mother and learning to say no, discovering our personal boundaries and separateness. We must repent of having sabotaged that progress by dishonest or ungraceful use of "no" and "yes."

Obedience

In the moral responsibility decision we experience a moral demand, the source of all obligation and morality. We must repent of any subversion of our being sons and daughters of the Father. The Five Decisions to be well are a way of life not, one-time events. We find we are continually having to make an honest searching spiritual and moral inventory of our lives.

Faith, Love and Hope - The Kingdom Plateau

The faith, love and hope decision comes by putting the first four decisions to work in our relationships. We must repent of specific issues and misbehaviors in our lives of goals that are not God's goals. We are to love our neighbor as Christ has loved us freely and without condition. There is a legitimate self-love because we are to love our neighbor as ourselves. This love is defined by Jesus in John 13:34, "As I have loved you, that you love one another, " is the kind of love that draws one's neighbor into its circle at the expense of our comfort. Godly self-love rests the self in the hand of God, not in the circumstances about one's self. What better love could I show for myself than to put myself into the hand of God, not in the circumstances about one's self. What better love could I show to others, than to invite and make room for them to join me. Spiritual growth and healing require working through deeper levels of truth, dependency and obedience. To have deeper experiences of our selfhood in Christ is to rise to the Kingdom Plateau when we discover the loveliness of people and the creation around us. Rising to the Kingdom Plateau is inheriting the earth. We work through deeper experiences of our freedom and responsibility and our righteousness in Christ building from the bottom up.

THE GROWTH OF PERSONAL FREEDOM

The Fifth Decision, trying to love people with the love of God, without the first four decisions being established will result in grief, frustration and cynicism.

Because am not a full person in Christ, I can only love when the first four decisions have developed in my life. If I have not put myself under the authority of God, my moral commitment and obligation to love my neighbor won't be there. Without the prior decisions, my love for neighbor will come and go with my comfort and convenience level because I have not yielded my self-at-the-center to Christ-at-the-center. If I have not taken responsibility for my behavior, attitudes and reactions, if I have not come to that decision to let my "no" be "no" and my "yes" be "yes," then my obedience to the Father will be unstable. I must first be an honest person before my commitment to the moral authority of the Father will have serious meaning. I must decide to be a real person before I can be a real person for Christ. "Behold an Israelite indeed, in whom is no guile." (John 1:47). It is the maturity of my personal integrity that gives meaning to our commitment to Jesus. If I have not placed my dependency on a foundation that can bear the weight of my being, I will not be able to take responsibility for my actions, excusing myself and blaming others to protect and defend the insecure selfhood not rooted in God, rooted only in the circumstances around me. If I have not committed myself to the truth or have betrayed that commitment I will be in a weak position to seek and to find where I can rest my dependency. I will be the blind victim of the false gods and goddesses of the world which claim to meet my needs, heal my hurts and give me riches.

The truth can be used destructively to beat people over the head, to hammer them with guilt, to deceive and to manipulate. To ensure that truth-seeking leads to love, decisions two, three and four need to be made. If I have trouble in my life, no victory over the world, flesh and the devil, trouble growing up spiritually and emotionally, If can't love my neighbor, spouse, children, parents and the boss, I need to check The Five Decisions and go back to start with number one.

Ask yourself, "Am I really interested in the truth? Is my dependency in God? Am I willing to take responsibility in our relationships and reject false guilt? Am I under the authority of God in our relationships? Have I made an honest commitment to love my neighbor as Christ loves me?" We need the light of logic to flush ignorance, brokenness and rebellion out into the light. We are designed to be open to the truth, designed to be dependent on God and are designed to love one another. Not pursuing those decisions, our being will be eroded and attacked.

Parenting and Children

Good skills begin with our parents in order to become a child of God and to be a successful child. Out goal in life is to become a child in God by obeying the fifth commandment to "Honor your father and mother." The Five Decisions are a good start and should be taught to our children. Each decision is a preparation for childhood in God, which will lead to adulthood in the world. As soon as the child can absorb teaching, we are to model our own childhood to God in the presence of the child.

Irreducibly Complex has been popularized by a professor in his arguments for ID intelligent design as opposed to Darwinian's evolution. A mouse trap will only work if all the pieces are together. If a part is missing, it won't work. Using this concept, if any steps of The Five Decisions is missing or defective in a person's life, that life will not work. We evolve from younger to older, from immature to mature. This requires intelligent design from both inside and outside. God is guiding the whole process. We must have parents who are intelligently obedient to the plan of God, and we must intelligently cooperate with discipleship. The process of reaching spiritual maturity requires all five steps (decisions). If any of the steps are missing or defective, the personhood will be immature or non-functional. The final product is to be an intelligent designer, with covenant (promises) choices of building Kingdom quality relationships. Then all the steps must come into place. This is a description of how intelligent designers are themselves intelligently created. Progress toward personhood requires three intelligent designers; a mothering and a fathering figure and the child. The successful evolution of one's personhood takes place by the intelligent design of parent and child. We evolve to the point where God takes over the parental roles in the progress of salvation. The evolution of intellectually, morally and spiritually mature individuals does not happen by chance or accident, God is behind it.

Clarification of the Christian faith and The Five Decisions are a statement of the Covenant relation with God. The decisions takes us through the normal growth process into the Kingdom and are also a healthy maturation into the Kingdom. These decisions are interdependent, they only work together. It is all the decisions together or nothing. We choose ourselves in or out of the Kingdom, under the amazing law and grace of God.

The starting point and foundation of the spiritual process is Decision #1. God wants us to worship Him, only if He really is God and if we honestly believe that He is God. Christianity is committed to the truth and is not subversive to the truth like secular people say. We don't obey God because the Big Meanie in the sky will beat us up if we don't; it's the world that will beat us up, not God. Dependence and obedience to God ensures us safety from the self-destructive world. The world will beat up anyone, even its own who take truth seriously. The world will reject and crucify anyone who makes The Five Decisions to be whole and well because that contradicts its power struggle and autonomy. The world is against those who are morally accountable, who love the truth unconditionally, because it can't tolerate reality or love.

The Five Decisions to Be Well are life or death decisions. If we make them, we will live, and if we don't make them we will die. Individuals and communities must make these decisions. Some say Rome fell because of immorality or because the Christians undermined Rome, but it fell because Rome refused to align itself with the purpose of God for the cosmos. The American Constitution states that religion must be separated from government. Separation from Church and State is poor logic, poor religion and poor politics. This is not what the founding fathers and the majority had in mind. Any culture including America that refuses to have a commitment to God and understanding The Five Decisions will sooner or later fall. No community can survive (including us) without God. Eroding societies breed eroding citizens. The biblical answer to the Five Decisions are a formulation of the covenant (promises) commitment between God and His people. If our foundation is not rooted in the truth, the whole truth, and nothing but the truth, everything else we build on that foundation will be suspect and will compromise the basic biblical teaching that we live by faith.

Faith means the risk of openness to the truth, a teachable spirit. The biblical claim that we are saved by faith must mean that we are saved by our full openness to reality. It is not sufficient simply to be open to truth but that is prerequisite of all that follows. For each of the decisions, God has committed Himself omnipotently, omnisciently, omnipresent and eternally into that relation with us.

1. He is offering us nothing but truth. John 8:32, "If you abide in my word you are truly my disciples."
2. He guarantees a firm substantial and dependable foundation for our lives. John 17:2, "The Father has given him power over all flesh to give eternal life."
3. God binds Himself to His Word Isaiah 55:4, "The Word of God will stand forever."
4. God is under no authority higher than Himself; no one is commanding Him
5. God is committed to love His creation regardless of how we behave. Romans 5:8 "God shows His love for us that while we were yet sinners Christ died for us."

The incarnation of the son gives us His truth and makes Himself known to His fallen people and to be truth seekers. God is calling us to Abandon the world, the flesh and the devil to enter into a relationship with Him. The world rejects anyone who makes The Five Decisions, or makes the Decisions and loves the world. The end goal of life is the family of God. We seek to imagine the truth, depend on it, and love it to make progress into maturity, wholeness and holiness.

Some Diagnostics Help - Moral and Spiritual Inventory

Decision-making takes place in the area of the conscious, mind and will. Therapist try to give care to hurts before assessing the person's intellect, moral and spiritual condition. They don't have a clear sense of spirituality. It is impossible to provide care before taking an inventory of his ability to behave rationally, morally and spiritually. Accomplishing The Five Decisions can provide a step in assessing the spiritual and emotional condition of the person if there is a need for inner healing. Those who have not considered the Five Decisions out of ignorance and stubbornness will find that emotional problems will begin to resolve as those decisions are made. Reliable knowledge and honest moral decision making are stabilizing and healing in and of themselves.

Emotional and Spiritual health requires an active faith relationship with reality, both listening to hear the truth and speaking to share the truth. Emotional and Spiritual disease will come with the sin of not hearing and not speaking the truth. Sin will cut any effort at emotional and spiritual growth. Sin is encountered in the heart of religious communities and traditions, surrounding themselves with all paraphernalia of religiosity without true spiritual power and authority. People create their own problems through their behavior and attitude. A "tough love" therapy by assessing the behavior of the person, to help inner areas of hurt, in order to not make it worse, need to look at. the maturity level. of the person conscious moral and spiritual life before getting sidetracked analyzing unconscious feelings, seeking hidden motives, trying to solve problems that are not there.

The therapy dealing with the unconscious moving back to the conscious and rational level is the goal of therapy, restoring to the person his ability to deal rationally, righteously and consciously. In a marriage, the counselor will ascertain the level of conscious commitment of both parties to the fullness of a Godly pattern for Christian marriage. Assuming too much about a person's understanding or commitment will happen when the therapist lacks spiritual authority and willingness to challenge the client. Some problems are due to unconscious and hidden negative emotions.

Problems can be solved by an understanding of the personal commitment to friendship between two persons and marriage relations. People can be helped by knowing the goals they have in life and their religious commitment, Godly goals and spiritual maturity. "How do my goals, attitudes and behaviors measure up along side of Jesus?" These factors influence our ability for emotional health. Sin is always an impediment to wholeness; sin is part of the problem to deal with. God has provided the solution; confess, repent and be forgiven. It is not easy, but it is simpler than healing brokenness without God and makes the healing more accessible. Trying to heal hurts in an unrepentant heart will cause the healing to become unglued and will create a more competent sinner. We do no favors by avoiding the sin issue. We need to challenge the goals and visions of the people with the vision of the Kingdom of God. The work of the Holy Spirit is to change their minds, not the therapist. It is the work of the therapist to challenge persons with the vision of the Kingdom and to help set them free to make a choice.

The emotionally disabled person will often judge truth and reality in a self-centered manner using his feelings to do so. Truth is bigger than our personal feelings. People who have a "victim" attitude toward life are not open to the truth and are not happy. All neurosis comes from poor relationships. We can choose to work through our pain or live a life in misery.

Track Record

A Christian's spiritual life with no discipline, no confession and no repentance has no backbone. A Christian, when helping someone, need not fear to raise the moral and spiritual issues on the grounds that religion is "private," prayer is unprofessional, or that a person will not want to deal with those issues. Part of one's healing and maturing requires identifying those areas when one is not willing to be honest and open. The one being helped has to make his own choice, but the choice and challenge must be presented. Only then can he say he was given a choice.

We don't have to demand a choice from them; if its a moral issue it can be kept in the back burner and dealt with to have a successful conclusion to spiritual growth. Discipleship and spiritual direction are used to strengthen the person, unless he is not willing to deal with the moral issues. The truth seeker is dealing with moral and spiritual issues. Truth-seeking is essential for being whole and well, a truth of which government has deprived it from schools and church schools. Helping persons with a long history of sin, rebellion, addiction need more time to have a good spiritual track record of healing and repentance before they announce themselves as healed and free. The old ways will come back, "Do not take anyone down off the cross until the Lord does." Love is free, but trust has to be earned only by a track record. It is not loving to pamper, it's a betrayal by the therapist if he does that. It looks like an improvement of good behavior, but sin is only on the surface.

There is a difference between repentance and wising-up to make changes in one's life so that one's behavior is not self-destructive but still self-centered. They can successfully be self-centered rather than self-destructive. People who are good at telling others are experts at this. Does therapy for criminal solve their criminality or will it turn neurotic and diseased criminals into more competent and well adjusted criminals? It's an issue unsolved.

Therapy without attending to moral and spiritual commitment will produce a well-adjusted worldling who are insulated from real spiritual needs. A significant track-record helps to recognize honest healing and repentance from just "faking it" or wising-up.

Moving From Discipleship Into Healing

By a Christian sense of health and wholeness, we can detect sickness. We are made in the image of God. Jesus is the son of God and therefore the image of God becomes imaginable. Jesus is our standard of health and the two great commandments point to health. The Five Decisions put concreteness in our spiritual lives and spiritual progress. A spiritual and moral inventory is the first thing to do when therapy begins. With the life of Christ and the word of God together with the therapist's knowledge to make progress. For a damaged, psyche we need reconstruction work to get us back on track of normal spiritual and emotional growth. At times our maturity and wholeness do not progress and we don't get anywhere because stress and inner malfunctions prevents us from it. Paul says we fail to do what we want and do what we do not want. Some say because we are new creatures in Christ all we have to do is pray, read scripture, have Christian fellowship and our inner distress and contradictions can be wished away or "Scripture quoted" away. It is not that simple; sometimes psychology and inner healing are needed. We must live the life as directed by Scripture. To admit contradictions is not lack of faith in God, it is to find that by that very faith we can bring those inner contradictions also to God. It's our evangelical calling to evangelize, teach and baptize those deep unconscious and secret areas that haven't heard the gospel. We turn to those blocks and ways of being released. The Healing Alliance for wholeness, holiness and the logic of Dependency. A tussle with Christians those who see repentance for sin and those who see healing of our brokenness. Both healing and repentance are needed. we must learn which one.

In the fallen world there will be both sin and brokenness. That part of me which is not whole cannot be holy. Wholeness is the substance of holiness, it is the whole of me that is to become holy. l am to be wholly dedicated to God. Wholeness and holiness are our two basic dependencies for being made in the image of God. We depend on God for our being, we depend on God for direction and also our moral dependencies. Christians have a faith relation with God out which our lives flow. Our lives flow not only from God, but from each other to communities and nations. God is not just an idea or an illusion existing only in the mind, God is a living reality, the Creator of all the world whose children we are, one can experience no deeper or more powerful affirmation of selfhood. The therapist and the client are being "reparented" as the damaged internal images of mothering and fathering area healed into health and lifesaving state. The therapist may be attempting something which only God can do. We can't depend on the world as a parent to become an adult. because the world cannot set us free from itself. The world will make me and adult-child-of-the-world, a compromised adult, because I will always be dependent on the world to supply my needs, the part of the world that's parenting me. I will never be an adult. Only with God can you be a full adult. This is why we have to be born again and be a child of God. In order to see the Kingdom of God we have to be full adults in God.

To be "born again" is to become a child dependent of God, no longer dependent on the world. Nicodemus would no longer rely on his Jewish identity as being a son of Abraham to complete his spiritual journey. He would become a son of God who does the final re-parenting. When we understand the logic of dependency we can understand the logic of Salvation. We don't need revelation or illumination from God for this. Our alliance must be established with God not with any human being.

The world is a dead-end because it can't raise up real adult persons who can stand emotionally and spiritually independent of the circumstances of life. Our alliance and bonding of faith relationship with God in whom we can rest our dependency independently from the world.

The Three Meanings of Faith

Christians have for twenty centuries taught the doctrine of salvation by faith. In the first three centuries, they experienced a more powerful spiritual renewal with a few exceptions of spiritual renewal. The meaning of faith was altered in the following years. Christians in the first three centuries would have looked at our present day faith as being out of touch with reality and contrary to "real" scientific knowledge. Early Christians understand themselves to be in touch with reality. Faith did not have the secular scientific humanism in the first three centuries to captivate their minds as we have today.

Secular humanism was known to the early Greek Philosophers, but it did not yet have the power and authority over man's mind which now does with the addition of "science the scientific method." In the middle centuries, there was a split between faith and "real" knowledge as philosophers asked, "What is the nature of reality?" The biblical revelation was strongly influenced, diluted and contaminated by the power of Greek philosophy. Greek philosophy had a lot to offer, but it was no match to the God-given knowledge and wisdom of the Hebrews. Philosophy refined their intellectual tools for discovering the truth for many centuries and giving explanation to the nature of the cosmos. Intellectual tools are helpful, but the Hebrews had access to the One who created the cosmos. Christians avoid the philosophical discussions since the times of the Renaissance and the Enlightenment of Europe where it started. In the twentieth century, the Christian community was not where you go for clear thinking about the issues of life. If we are saved by grace, we need to meet the challenge of secularism successfully. But faith was regulated to "religion" and human nature was regulated to secular psychology.

The word salvation is "fullness of health, wholeness, joy and integrity." This touches our physical, emotional and spiritual lives, integrating them into unity. From Genesis to Revelation the Bible teaches that the physical realm is to be a sacrament, an outward and visible sign of the spiritual and that God is redeeming the physical from its fallen state. The sacramental split between the physical and spiritual does not exist. The split came from Greek and other pagan philosophy and religion and became very evident in the Church by the middle ages. To make sense of salvation by faith, we need to have the concept of faith. We need a concept of faith which is compatible with us being ourselves and having relationship. It is the basic foundation of ourselves and of our relationships. If this is not so, talk about salvation by faith will be superstition and jargon.

Four Decisions of Faith

There are three meanings to the word "faith." I personally trust; I trust you with my wallet, because I know you are honest. Faith is what you do when you run out of evidence or arguments, you just believe anyhow. Faith is a blind leap. The willingness to risk being wrong even if the evidence is not there; even if it's contrary to what one believes. Faith is "openness to the truth," a willingness and openness to experiencing the truth and reasoning honestly about that experience.

Faith has three meanings:
A. Personal Trust
B. Intellectual or Creedal Commitment
C. Blind Leap.

What ties everything together is "openness to the truth." The willingness and openness to experiencing the truth and reason honestly about that experience.

Four Decisions of Faith:
1. Openness to the Truth,
2. Personal Trust
3. Intellectual or Creedal Belief
4. Blind Leap.

The first two of the Five Decisions leading to freedom and wholeness combined are called the "Faith-Dependency Relationship" that forms the basis of the spiritual life. It is only by faith, openness to the truth that I can risk a dependency relationship. If I choose to be open to the truth, I can form a dependency relationship, which is the basis for a healthy life. The Spiritual life is the key to integrating my wholeness "Your faith has made you whole" (Luke 8:48). This is not intellectual faith, but openness of spirit, a teachable heart that I perceive in you to be healed and allows them to be touched when they come into the presence of truth. Faith as personal trust and intellectual commitment depend on being open to the truth.

One who is not open to the truth will not know who to trust or what to believe and rely only in the blind leap. The bling leap is a faith we engage in when we do no know what else to do. Some believe God honors blind faith more than reasonable faith, that blind faith proves our trust in Him more fully. This is not what the Bible teaches.

No matter how much evidence and experience we get, there is always room for doubt in our decisions. There is always a question we can ask. There is a degree of blindness in our decisions. Every decision is to some degree a blind leap, for there a no infallible people among us. If I am living by Decision #1 - The Decision of Faith, I will gain experience to know who I can trust and who I can't trust. I am leaping into the Light. The more we live by Faith Decision #1 (Openness to the Truth), the more my Faith #2 (Personal Trust and Intellectual Belief) grows and the less we will have to depend on Faith #4 (The Blind Leap). Leaping blindly is a virtue you do. only when necessary. Sometimes we must make a decision when we don't have all the evidence, but leaping blindly when not necessary is stupidity. If I am not living by faith (not open to the truth), I will take a blind leap into the dark. Life will feel like a void that brings fear and anxiety.

If I am living by faith by being open to the truth of God then decision #4, the blind leap, will not be into the dark; it will be a leap into the light. The void will turn into hope that will conquer fear and anxiety. The leap into the light is a leap toward relationship. God's light includes persons because they are the fundamental realities of the cosmos.

If Jesus is the Way, the Truth and the Life, then on the journey of faith, looking into the future we can see the face of someone coming to meet us and a Family to which we am called to. How I experience the risk of Faith #4 (the blind leap) into a void of darkness or light will depend on the quality of faith #1 that I exercise. Faith #4, the blind leap, means there will always be a risk. Life is a personal experience, and God (who is also personal) gives us meaning. If life is not personal where God is not personal (who does not give us meaning to our lives), the impersonality of the world will win over us by default.

Faith and Operational Truth - The Gap Between Appearance and Reality

How do we know when we have the truth or false appearance of truth? In the woods, at a distance, is it a rock or is it a bear. In practice, we try to discern truth by observation and reasoning. The definition of truth is "as it really is" or "what is" reality. Knowing the definition of a word does not give the content for that word. We still don't know how to describe reality. Western culture says that "science" has all the answers that the scientific method tells us the real truth about things. Science is defined as rules of evidence which can be used publicly that leads to Truth in a given area. The two aspects of science are observation and reason, and are also the foundations of biblical Faith #1.

There is no difference between what Christians do in believing in God as to what scientists do as they discover quasars. Science runs by faith in the same sense that biblical belief runs by faith. The difference is the subject which uses different rules of procedure for proving or disproving a theory.[13] Faith is given to each area to separate science and gives us the rules of evidence that leads to truth. We run into truth when we follow this rules. The rules define the "operational" definition of "what is" of reality.

Faith is the willingness to risk the unknown (a blind leap) on the basis of the known (Decisions #1-3). We begin "where we are" with what we do understand and use the clues at hand to proceed further into reality. There is no other way to learn in any field of

---

[13] Behe, Michael J. *Darwin's Black Box: The Biochemical Challenge to Evolution.* New York: Simon & Schuster, 1998. Print.

knowledge. To bump into reality, we learn to seek and to speak the truth. We seek truth and speak in love, so there is cooperation rather than competition from those around us. There is nothing more significantly maturing and healing than being dedicated to truth. That is why Jesus told us that the truth would set us free. We are saved (introduced to reality) by our faith, being fully in reality is the same as being saved.

The Healthy Soul comes by making the five decisions that lead to health, wholeness and freedom. The faith journey. includes all four aspect of faith, being open to truth, having personal trust, intellectual belief, and taking a blind leap. The Soul is made up of a mind (head) a will (heart) and the emotions (bowels), the inner adult, child and parent thanks to Transactional Analysis TA.[14] The head symbolizes our conscious adult intellectual awareness. The head can stand independently on its own, assess situations, act intelligently and rationally. The adult looks to the future with a special virtue of hope. The adult part of us is the authority (inside) in relation to the child in us. The adult in us needs to take authority over the child within. The heart symbolizes our child-like side, including dependency decision making and focuses on the present with special virtues of trust, obedience and love. The child is the foundation for the adult and also the emotional foundation. Disruption between the child and adult sides causes sickness.

A few strong men went down into a shaft to rescue a little girl that had fallen in. When they heard her cry they had to stop working, because they cried also. There is something about a child that touches and resonates with the child within each of us. Sometimes the child within ourselves is locked up in a dungeon or fallen into an emotional mine shaft.

---

[14] Harris, Thomas A. *I'm OK, You're OK; a Practical Guide to Transactional Analysis.* New York: Harper & Row, 1969. Print.

CHAPTER SIX: THE DAMAGED SOUL

The soul is the mind. will and emotions or bowels.[15] In John 3:17, John wrote whoever "Seeth his brother have a need and shutteth up his bowels of compassion from him how dwelleth the love of God in him." From the Hebrew point of view, the bowels are one of the centers of emotional life. They are our early memories are images of our mother and father. The bowels are a storehouse of past memory and are the residence of the parent side of ourselves. From the child's point of view, the parent is the God figure; the place of ultimate dependency. This is why parenting is so determinative in a child's life and so often needs restructuring. My childhood in God is the foundation for my adulthood in the world. To achieve that deep reparenting, redeemed God images will be required. The special virtue of the bowels is faith; the stability of having bonded with reality which comes from accumulation of experience with truth, stored away in our bowels.

Faith is that ground of past experience upon which we stand as we deal with the present and look to the future. Strong faith comes out of strong parenting which models for us the four levels of faith. The maturity of our adult, child, and parents represents St.

---

[15] Janov, Arthur. *The Primal Scream: Primal Therapy: The Cure for Neurosis*. New York: Putnam, 1970. Print.

Paul's triad of faith, hope and love; the three that endure (1 Corinthians 13). Jesus is the Child-in-God, and became The Adult-in-The World. In the world, there is no stabile adulthood. The bowels represent the foundation for child and adult in the sense that the bowels represent the unconscious area of life, the subterranean places and the ground of our being; our Diaphragm, Hands and Feet. In the healthy soul, there is open communication in the soul. The head, heart and bowels are opened to each other. There is no built-in separation. The unconscious is a place of light and supports the conscious. It is not dark hostile, dangerous or undermining.

The feet represent our dependency, contact with reality, with the ground of our being, and the ability to be ourselves. It is the spiritual ground on which we stand. The expressions, "Get your feet on the ground," "He has cold feef" "My knees are knocking!" "I am on shaky ground" "Someone pulled the rug from under me" "You are skating on thin ice." All of these indicate nervousness. On the other hand, "I feel like I am on solid ground" indicates strength in a situation.

I can "be me." We experience our feet on solid ground when we are open to reality. Jesus tells us to build our houses on the Rock, not the sand. Like the hymn says "All other ground is sinking sand." Our feet have to be firmly planted in relationship reality. The ground of which is our relationship for being our very existence. The trinity of thinking-willing-feeling needs to be understood as a thinking-willing relationship, for feelings are relationship knowledge. The will is the bridge between thinking and relationship. The will chooses to act or not on what the mind knows, engaging or not in relationships, creating feelings and emotions. In the healthy soul all of these aspects of ourselves work in harmony. are not pulled in different directions by internal strife.

When I make a decision, I make it with the whole of me. The adult, child, parent, masculine, and feminine are working as one. I am an integrated "put together" person.

The Deepest Damage

Because of our defensiveness to the openness of truth, our dependency relations cannot mature. The deepest damage within us as we build our Kingdom of self is to our faith-dependency relation because it cannot mature. It starts, first with our parents and then with our Parent. It is the failure of parenting and of child-like behavior to traverse the Five Decisions to be me, to be a whole person a mature lover of souls on the Kingdom Plateau.

The normal means of maturation do not suffice so healing intervention is required. Those first two basic decisions of our spiritual life, truth and dependency don't get off the ground or are aborted in our growth. Something prevents us from living out open relation to the truth and that upon which we can safely rest our dependency.

The damage takes place at a level that we can't control and is very difficult and painful to heal. The failure undermines the success of the other three decisions. We are unable to be open and honest and commit to obedience to God or to be lovers of souls. The deepest damage is not caused by the pain and hurt, it is caused by our reaction to the hurt. Our tendency is to find a scapegoat for our illness leads us to believe that our "put-downs" we attain in life have been what puts us down. How we handle the put-downs will determine how deeply and long-term the damage is sustained in our souls. This is good news because it puts us back in charge of our lives. There is very little we can do about being victims of the fallen-world, unless there is something beyond blaming the world. We ourselves can do a spiritual inventory of our behavior and it may be painful to our egos, but it gives us back authority and control over our lives.

A Picture of the Damaged Soul

The head, heart and bowels of a damaged soul are different from a a healthy soul. The head is inflated. It indicates the (intellectually strong) ego that lives in their heads in a world of abstraction. The heart is resting on the top of a cork which seals off the bowels (the storehouse of feelings) from the more conscious levels of mind and will. Our ontological feet are withered and retracted, not on solid ground of personal relationship. They do not stand on the eternal ground of being, the Hand of God and feels as if suspended over a void. The term "feet" is a metaphor. We are talking about our dependency on God.

We created beings have an external ground of our being. "Feet" is a metaphor to express that dependency. We understand how we put our feet on solid ground in the world. How do we "feel" if our ontological dependency secure or insecure? There is a healthy dependency of being. If feels warm like the comfort an infant feels in the mothers arms. A comfort one feels with the whole of one's being; not with a part of ourselves. There is security in the relationship. But some- times we do not. Suppose that in our childhood we had the trauma of an abusive father who would beat up all the family and this affected us emotionally.

The two-year-old child's identity comes from the bad father. When the Father beats up the child, it's not only the father that is bad, but also God. The world comes crashing down on the child. Life becomes destructive with no place to hide. This event is to dramatize a point. Small hurts accumulate over a long period of time. Maybe a trauma didn't happen. A lack of affirmation from the parents may have developed a "deprivation neurosis" (rather than a trauma neurosis). When something happens or fails to happen, it is beyond our ability to deal with it. We tend to deny that it happened. We want to forget it and hope it will go away. We want to shove the memory down into our bowels, put the cork on the bottle and seal it up from ever reaching us again. We repress the memory. This is one way we separate feelings from relationships. We try to build a world of good feelings apart from relationships. Good feelings do not exist without God. God does not want us to sneak good feelings apart from Him. The disbelief that God wants us to feel good leads to addictions.

After living this way, we confuse good feelings for good relations. Much if not most "falling in love" is a confusion of lust with love. "If it feels good, do it," becomes our primary moral principle. Such a principle becomes the very denial of all morality. When I bottle up a feeling or a memory, I am bottling up part of myself.

The two-year-old child is locked up in my memory, imprisoned with the bad father and God figure. A part of me is locked up into that relationship with my worst enemy. The child grew up and the alcoholic father repented, but the child at twenty-one still thinks the father is going to beat him up. At twenty-one he still acts like a two year old and cannot figure out why. He forgot that there is a two year old down in the bottle full of rage, resentment and guilt who manages to assert himself through the cork. When given the right spiritual resources, we can sustain hurt and pain and come out better than we went into it. The deeper damage occurs when in order to protect ourselves from our own feelings and reactions we put the cork on the bottle, splitting off a part of ourselves and preventing ourselves from acting as a unity. We become disintegrated. That part of me below the cork can no longer act in harmony with me above the cork.

We put ourselves down in reaction to the hurt and rejection. We reject a part of ourselves. Our defenses then damage us more than our hurt. How we react to the hurt causes more damage than the hurt from which they were meant to protect. It is our truth-testing ability. The faith decision is damaged. The two year old part of me is in a dungeon in my bowels. That part of me is out of touch with reality. The bottled up two-year-old is not able to grow in reality. It has been denied access to reality. It cannot learn that not all fathers are bad. Even after the father repented the child remains locked in an eternal struggle between itself and bad father. The cork is placed over the storehouse of feeling and emotions. The dependency relationship in which the person being depended on could not or would not meet the needs of the child. Because the child experiences his very identity being attacked, he will react by denying the reality of the dependency at all "If this is what being dependent gets me, I'll stop being dependent."

Faith-dependency is affected and the quest for isolated self-sufficiency rather than honest adult maturity begins. Getting well and whole requires the admitting and repenting of all those decisions to back-out of a relationship life. Infantile autonomy is the quest for autonomy driven by unmet dependency needs and destructive dependency relationships. If we do not repent of abandoning our relationship life, then we will be driven by our own quest for autonomy.

Relationship vs. autonomy often appear as the two basic choices of all life. The drive for autonomy can never work because we are dependent beings. We will always end up in healthy or unhealthy dependency. The compulsion for self-sufficiency can gain the status of a religion as evidenced by secular humanism and Eastern religions. Our childhood past is the source of our emotional distress.

Each new stage of life presents its own dependency situation, new threats to our personal integrity that can disrupt the faith-dependency relation and growth process and begin the failure aborting the journey perilous into individuation and adulthood. We are always dependent and the potential failure of our dependency relationships makes us vulnerable. The future can turn dark no matter how good the past has been. If the circumstances of our dependency turn dark, we may resort to our infantile autonomy at any time in our lives. That means again that the key to emotional health is our relation to God, not primarily to our parents. Natural infancy is meant to include Godly parenting. Adult circumstances may reduce us again to an infantile faith-dependency relation which can override our adult rational sensibilities if we are not very secure in our identity and sense of selfhood. In such circumstances, we can become dependent on captors or cult leader as a refuge from the slings and arrows of outrageous fortune. Or, we can fall apart because we can't find a substitute refuge from overwhelming reality. Life in the fallen world has a way of giving the lie to our imagined autonomy. The faith-dependency relationship is the rock bottom foundation which on all else in our lives is built. Sustaining and quality of that relation through hurt, pain and disappointment is paramount to our growth process. The only permanent solution is to build our house on the Rock which no worldly force can disturb. All other ground is sinking sand.

Metaphysics, Feelings and Relations

Relationships are Metaphysical. Life is about relationship. The two highest commandments in the cosmos are to love God and one another. Personal relationship drives us beyond the physical and phenomenal. It is our ability to discern the presence initially; our mother is a metaphysical capacity. We see beyond the merely physical and sensory body to a "someone." The crib is soft and pretty, but does not give life. It's the mother that gives life enhancement to the baby who can discern the mothers presence. Babies have the metaphysical capacity; it is inborn and natural. There is a "seeing," a perception beyond the five senses. Metaphysical perception is primordial and original. The spiritual life (personal relationship life) is the primary metaphysical experience and the primary mode of perception. When spiritual perception erodes, so does all the rest of life. The spiritual perception erodes and the perception of personal relationships erodes also. Apart from a secure spiritual grounding, nothing can sustain it from eroding. The creation story is that we are made in the image of God; male and female. Our personhood and our gender are discovered and sustained only as we are embedded in personal relationship, family and Holy communion.

Behaviorist philosophies are driven to explain personhood, but create a cosmos which is irrational and unlivable. People are merely random, accidental sparks generated by the collision of atoms. Without metaphysical entities, the soul, mind, will, feelings, and psychology would have nothing to study (and worse, no persons to do the studying).

Every scientist (as a knowing being) is a metaphysical entity. We cannot reduce souls and psyches to mere phenomenon. The reality of personal life is required to make sense. Phenomenal life goes into chaos if relationship dies. Without personal relationship we deteriorate because we can't make sense of our own experiences. the phenomena. That means that personal relationship is a metaphysical event, an event "meta" (beyond) the physical. It is impossible despite behaviorist's best efforts to reduce personhood to an impersonal phenomenon. The soul is not a phenomenal (one of the five senses) object. Persons are sacramental beings for whom the physical is an expression of the spiritual. Souls, non-perceivable objects, communicate through perceivable things are phenomena. The self reveals itself through the physical, as molecular biology and other sciences are discovering. The secular and pagan worlds are secular and pagan because of their defective metaphysical perception. They do not have a living relationship with God who created us and who is sovereign. They are lacking in personal relationship quality. Hindu and other cultures are imbedded in clan and family, but that is not consistent with their spirituality. It's against implications of impersonalism.

Health persons find ways of living above their philosophies and religions. In both the secular and pagan worlds, people are not entities (full adults), they are sons only in the Judeo- Christian cosmos. If we retain a small flame of personal relationship with someone, somewhere, somehow, there is still hope that our relation with God can be restored. That is the parable of the Last Judgement in Matthew 25. The erosion of relationship (C. S. Lewis) among those who choose hell over heaven, self and good feeling over the way of the Cross; the way of responsible relationship. Those on their way to hell decline God's answer to the Five Decisions and do not live by the four aspects of faith. They are not interested in the life of fullness and most marvelous of all realities that God is offering.

Once Burned, Twice Shy

We are born small, vulnerable and dependent in need of input from first mother and then father to get our identity. In this stage of life, parents are in the role of God. The power of being comes from the mother; power, authority and purpose for the infant comes from the father. Sometime the parents don't do a Godly job. When our power and authority relations go bad, it becomes hard to make the Five Decisions. When we get hurt deeply or disappointed, as an infant, we tend to put a wall between ourselves and the offending party. We emotionally withdraw. We pull back and put distance between ourselves and them, "defensive detachment." "Once burned twice shy." If we have painful feelings, we want to avoid future painful experiences with that person by distancing ourselves.

Defensive detachment. is a common strategy of self-protection. Such distancing is a metaphysical event. I am distancing myself from persons, other metaphysical entities beyond the phenomenal. When feelings are distanced from personal relationships, we are left with phenomena, erosion and a loss of that which makes the physical phenomenal world-sacramental (and meaningful). We can pull back from our relationships, but we take our feelings with us. Our feelings become separated from our relationship. If a feeling is relationship knowledge, then separation means something has seriously gone astray. Our feelings can no longer tell us accurately about our relationships. They become free-wheeling, self-contained entities in themselves and we pursue good feelings rather than relationships as though good feelings were the remedy for life. The defensive splitting has a price. In a healthy situation we fix bad feelings by fixing the relationship out of which it came. If we fear the relationship, we will avoid it by distancing ourselves. So to feel good we try to fix not the relationship but the bad feeling. We don't deal with the source of the bad relationships, we try to heal the symptom of pain by using drugs, sex, addictions, fame and power because they make us feel good without having to deal with difficulties of our relationships. Instead of relationship-building (a way to feeling good), we put our trust in mechanical means. Addictions are escapes from the hard work of relating and attempts to sugarcoat the pain and emptiness of relationship without taking responsibility for our end of the relationship. Sexualizing is making sexual pleasure a way of sugar-coating our brokenness and hurt. We can be intoxicated by alcohol, power, food, or fame while trying to make the emptiness of our defensive world tolerable and pleasant for a while. We can have Heaven with God or Hell all by ourselves.

There is a story of three people locked in hell who cannot get alone with each other. One of them said, "Hell is other people."[16] This remark sums up the attitude of world-denying religions which sees the world of individuality, personhood and relationship as the hell from which to escape.

The biblical view is different, holding personhood as the highest form of existence and the goal of all life to be relationship. No other religion or philosophy says that. The challenge of the Bible is before us, "choose this day whom you will serve," God or the kingdom of self. Choosing God means choosing relationship, because in the law of love, God made relationship the key to His Kingdom. We have a choice presented through Scripture and through our lives. We can build heaven (abundant life) with God by fixing bad relationships or Hell (disintegration and death) without fixing bad relationships all by ourselves with out God. Building by ourselves leads to hell because there is no life without God. Denying God is denying one's relationships when we are vulnerable as children. When we defensively detach from our parents, we are detaching from God. We do not want to be mothered or fathered by anyone. Pursuing good feelings rather than relation ships hinders each of the Five Decisions which are about building relationships. Feeling-good is the fallen world's "abundant life." That's why, "if it feels good, do it" makes sense to the fallen world. With this value system, we block out the person-hood at the other end of the relationship. We see that person not as a person, but as some-

---

[16] *No Exit*. By Jean-Paul Sartre. Théâtre Du Vieux-Colombier, Paris. 1944. Performance.

thing to make us feel good and judge the other persons worth by how he or she makes us feel. This is how abortion came about; the ultimate depersonalization was "legalized."

We live in a world of private feelings rather than real relationships; a world that is inherently self-centered. We are to love our neighbors as ourselves. We are to include the other end of the relationship with vigor equal to that which we devote to ourselves. We must include ourselves and the other or we will deny both the other and ourselves a relationship. We must allow the gift of each other to fully participate in any legitimate relationship. Only then can feelings function as they are meant to.

The casualty of this separate feeling from relationship is our personal relation with God that leaves as "on our own." We can no longer live by grace which exists only in relationship. We are plunged into the world, the flesh and the devil; a power struggle to control circumstances so that we can feel good. The damage to the faith-dependency relation is presented in Genesis 3; the story of the fall.

Adam and Eve lost their fundamental dependency relation with God and lost their openness to truth. This is shown by the fig leaves behind which they hid; symbols of our first defense mechanisms. They could no longer stand "naked and unashamed" before God or one another. In the next eight chapters the consequences of the separation work themselves out. When we distance ourselves from relationships, we cannot trust other persons. We must control them. We are not receiving gifts from them. we are extracting resources from them. Life without God is cannibalism. We eat each other up. This detachment affects our metaphysical, reality, and social life as we begin to close the circle of Uroboros around ourselves. The circle becomes a fortress. which we seek to decorate with pleasures experiences. Pleasure instead of good relationships becomes the goal of life. Relationships becomes the goal of life as tools for feeling good. A clinical description of the disaster which we bring upon ourselves.

The Three Steps Into The Fall

We first subvert the truth. We find something that is more valuable to us than the truth. If we have defensively detached, we subvert our relation to the most essentials of truth; the truths of relationship. Feelings will become more important than relating well. When our truth-seeking is compromised, we become confused about who God is and whether He is. Secondly our basic dependence must rest on some other foundation than the Hand of God. God says, "If on your own is what you want, on your own is what you will get." We get what we ask for. This leads to the third step in the Fall, putting our trust in false gods that will not meet our needs. Our confused soul and behavior become self-destructive, clinging to the idols that will not deliver what they promised. The separation of our feelings from our relationships is a definition of the Fall. We cast ourselves out of the world of responsible relationships into a world of desperate and willful searching for good feelings and of the power struggle to maintain them. The separation of feelings from relations destroys the sacramental nature of the universe, communion among spiritual beings through a physical universe. The Fall leads us either to materialism and pleasure-seeking into intellectualism and rationalism or spiritualism, all that see the cosmos as impersonal. The perennial philosophy, the philosophy of the fallen world, is the separation of feelings from relations because its built on a fundamental depersonalization of life. The Bible, on the other hand, sees the world built by an eternal and personal Somebody, not a thing, not a machine, an essence, a state of being or cosmic soup. Separation of feelings from relationship lead to a fallen worldview because it breaks the metaphysical relations. To choose relationship over self-centeredness is to move into the light to choose God. That is the message of the parable in Matthew 25 of the last judgement. The Kingdom of Heaven is all about relationship, and salvation is all about restoring our relationship with God and to relate to all, with anyone, in a substantial, real and helpful way. Loving God and neighbor the two highest commandments in the cosmos are about relationship.

The cross life is getting cleaned up for a relationship. Living by grace means putting our good feelings in the hands of another person. This is possible if we put ourself in the Hand of God first. None of these things focus on "feeling good" and may lead to deep pain and suffering. The paradox is that when we do it God's way, we do feel amazingly better compared to what the world can offer because God is full of grace and pours all the blessings of heaven and earth on us. But it comes as a gift not under our control, not earned and not owned. We cannot get the peace that passes understanding any way other than freely. We cannot pay for these gifts, we can't earn them, control or manipulate them. We have to give up our defenses and controls and get back into relationship to freely receive them. Salvation is God restoring us back into relationship from our self-isolation, from the hell of ourself. Life comes freely, gracefully and in relationship or not at all.

Disintegration of The Soul

Each of the three main parts of the soul can be deeply damaged by this splitting effect.

1. The head (or adult side of ourselves) tends to support the obsession for unrealistic self-sufficiency and autonomy. Thinking including the intellectually gifted tend to split off from feelings and to encourage schizoid approach to life. We tend to "live in our heads" to intellectualize and to drift further out of touch with concrete feeling and intuitive reality. The head or intellectual life tends to become inflated and "balloons" out of proportion. The forward looking virtue of hope tends to become abstract, unrealistic, "head in the clouds" and ungrounded in concrete reality or discouraged and hopeless. We can't live in our thoughts, we can only think our thoughts. The only place we can live is in relationship. This is what defenses are trying to prevent. In a healthy soul the intellect functions in concert with the will and feelings. In a damaged soul this is not the case.

2. The heart (or child side); When the split happens it tends to become willful and defensive. The virtues of love, justice and righteousness are turned to self-serving. The child rejects its own nature, that of being dependent, and takes the mind (the adult side) to become an independent, autonomous decision maker. The relationships turn into a power struggle. The relationships rooted in God is eternal. Decisions and thoughts are about relationships, not substitutes for them.

3. The bowels (the parent side) begin to be experienced as a place of conflict between self and the forces of the world represented by mother and father the storehouse of bad feelings. The domination of bad feelings fuels the obsession, for good feelings regardless of the relationship. The bowels become a pit, the dungeon or the void with Bad Mother and Bad Father in disguise. My fundamental gender images are at war entrapping the child in a closed system with no appeal to God who stands independently of the circumstances of the cosmos (A place in which the negative circumstances of life have the final word). Life is a bondage to Bad Mother and Bad Father, the Bad Gender images. There is a compromise between Good and Bad Parental images, but the good can never win over the bad in a world where the true God does not reign. The bad wins because of the irresolvable confusion.

4. The diaphragm instead of being open and connecting our storehouse of past memories and present, it becomes a cork between the heart and the bowels. It prevents the ventilation of those dangerous forces down below from erupting into the conscious life and disrupting those dependency relationships which still survive.

5. The ontological feet don't sense the reality feeling of the ground, the Hand of God upon which we rest. We deny our creature-hood because false closed-circle feet sprout on top of the cork. Our dependency is experienced as resting on the sea of chaos within Uroboros and the disruption repressed below in the bowels. Our inner turmoil becomes the "ground of our being." We experience reality in terms of our confusion projected onto the world around us. "All other ground is sinking sand."

6. Our hands and words symbolize our capacity to change things to affect the world. We construct narcissistic cosmos for ourselves to ease the pain in a hopeless world. When I try to give myself meaning, I hear only the empty echo of my loneliness.

CHAPTER SEVEN: REALITY VS. FREUD

The picture of the cosmos as sacramental images of persons is the opposite of secular psychology. The secular position is that "reality" is hard and unfriendly, but pleasurable. The goal is to capture and hang on to the pleasurable moments. The insecure child leaves the safe and comforting parental nest and longs for the protective parent-child relation that projects out to the universe to a God who is a father to him.

According to Sigmund Freud (secular) is our universal obsessive neurosis, the root of religion. Freud felt himself as a child of the scientific age rooted in scientific reasoning disproving the reality of God. The truth is neither science or man's wisdom has accomplished such a feat. Freud was disastrously wrong. The problem is not man's yearning for safety in an unfriendly world as Freud maintained, rather it is his defenses erected against painful failures of the faith-dependency relation that prevent him from having a relation with the very God that he says we project into the universe. God alone can resolve our inner loneliness brokenness and pain.

The damaged soul cannot keep the two primary decisions to seek to live in the truth and rest one's dependency on the only safe place it can be rested; in God. We can be damaged goods at anytime we are dependent and feel let down. The deepest hurt and damage occur when we are small and undeveloped emotionally and intellectually, while still identifying with our parents and others around us for our identity and well-being. We can become fragmented as strife and competition evolve in our head, heart and bowels (or between adult, child and parent). The tragic occurrence of multiple personality disorder is related to such fragmentation. Until these, of ourselves we will have a mutual respect for each other. We will never be able to function as whole persons. The hope of salvation from such damage must include determination to pursue all five of those decisions to be well and openness to the grace of God to fulfill them. Anything not yet fully whole cannot yet be fully holy. It is short of the perfection for which it is created.

The Unholy Alliance and The Failure of The Cork: Un-Whole and Unholy

The psyche in this disintegrated state works to make up for the deficits created by the split situation while the conscious part of the circumstances defensively try to pull together. The heart and head the two parts of the soul and bowels are available for cooperation. Even in the most devastating of emotional splits, some residue of feelings and relationship will remain. There is a sizable amount of emotional life accessible to consciousness. The head and heart tend to see bowels as the place of danger. The mind sizes up the situation and realizes that the disruptive feelings in the bowels are not to be loosed, or repercussions will result that come (usually) from the parents. If the raging child deep down in us were to act out its feelings, the child would get spanked, sent to their room or punished. So the heart (or will) with the knowledge of the head chooses to keep those feelings under wraps.

An unholy alliance develops between the head and heart to control the feelings. The alliance is unholy because it works directly against the faith dependency relationship in which we alone can't find wholeness and the substance of holiness. It is by nature a rejection of dependency and inhibits the openness to the truth that is the fundamental requirement of wholeness. It's an unholy alliance not leading to wholeness or holiness. The soul is cut off from a secure faith dependency relationship. Now, it is trying to make the best of a bad situation in a world where there is no secure and loving dependency relationship; trying to deal with a broken dependency relationship in a Godless world. Without God, it will not work. A world that offers no secure dependency relationship cannot sustain the kind of faith-dependency relation required for spiritual and emotional maturity. There is disruption also in the physical realm, which is the sacrament of the spiritual. This leads to death, or the Fall. The self enters self-sufficiency, rejecting the dependency relationship or if it is stuck with another person, it will manipulate them to keep them under control. This decline into darkness and chaos is part of the Fall found in Genesis 3:2, a condition reflected in most pagan mythology known to us. The cork is experienced as the platform upon which one stands, floating over the sea of chaos beneath. The cork is not the solution to the problem; it only suppresses the problem. The cork remains in place because there is nothing except God to heal the damage done to the past dependency relationships or to redeem the destructive God-image created in the mind of the child. There is no God-figure available in the world to help the hurting child with the Bad Parent to protect the child.

    The Head and Heart will not allow the unconscious and repressed memories to ascend or descend to deal with them (Freudian). The repressed child remains in bondage to the Bad Father and Bad mother and the drive toward self-sufficiency becomes compulsive. This bondage relationship is projected out onto the world and becomes as Freud noted, our father and mothers pasted onto the cosmos. The relationship is reflected in the ancient world through pagan myths. This characteristic is seen in pagan religions. This is also reflected in modern ways through our attachments to our worldly goods and power structures with the illusion that we have "come of age," and we are in control of our destinies. Are pagan religions our father and mother images that are projected onto the universe? (Sigmund Freud)

Biblical religion does not fall into this. The Unreliable Cork in our emotional life brings trouble to us from being open to the truth. The cork does not cure the situation but only hides it. There is danger when the forces under the cork will pop the cork out. The eruption of those unfriendly and troublesome feelings. A two-year-old may plant a cork and successfully withstand the emotional storm below the cork by getting along with the parents and friends, going to school, leaving home, marrying and getting a career. But the stresses of a job and marriage will drain his energy, he would wonder why a thirty-year-old person acts like a two-year-old; because when he was small, he put a cork on his bad feelings and later tries to get out. Now he is fighting a war on two fronts; an inner war (repressed feeling) trying to get out. It is a war with the unconscious and the outside war with the circumstances of life. He may experience burnout or emotional breakdown. When his guard is down, when he says, "I've had it with the job, with the family, because the two-year-old locked up for so long is now older and bigger and more dangerous than before." Guilt is something that's repressed in the unconscious, but it will affect a person's surroundings with painful thoughts and feelings like a body that floats. It will affect their surroundings with painful thoughts and feelings, like the stench of a floating body. (John G. Price). Corks are not leak proof in all of us. There will be some seepage past the cork of the frustration below. This seepage will affect our attitude and behavior in the world around us. It will drain our sense of joy and peace and prevent us from investing ourselves fully and joyfully into our relationships. Our division will make it impossible for us to live either whole or holy lives. The frustrations below the cork are the cause of nightmares, anxiety. depression, phobias and other plagues. Because we have locked these feelings into the unconscious of our bowels, it keeps us immature and out of touched with reality, unable to grow, be corrected or mature. Our real testing is blocked and blind spots are built into the psyche, preventing us from experiencing the freedom of an open and honest faith-dependency relationship.

The Holy Alliance, The Faith Commandment and Childing

In the process of growth, the adult meets Jesus, a personal relation develops. Something new comes; the experience of a dependency relationship with God in whose image we are made, the King of Kings and the Lord of Lords, the resurrected Messiah at whose name every knee shall bow and every tongue confess that He is Lord . "Jesus" in Hebrew means "Yahweh saves" or "I Am saves." God gave Himself the name "I Am" with Moses at the burning bush. "I Am" is a statement of absolute individuality, personhood, and uncreated being. We can say "I am" also only because "He is." My existence is always a dependent upon His existence. Only the existence of God is uncreated and self-sufficient, only God can say "I am." Because Jesus is, as Christians say, the Son of God, the personal Self-disclosure of the Father. When I meet Jesus, I am meeting Yahweh I Am. John. 14:9 Jesus is talking to Philip. "He who has seen me has seen the Father how can you say show us the Father." Jesus becomes my Lord and Savior from whom I receive my direction and goals. A new alliance forms as the head and heart commit to Jesus a holy alliance that can lead to wholeness and holiness because He who is both whole and holy is now the coach of my soul and sitting on the throne of my spiritual center. The holy alliance is the healing alliance. For the first time in my life, I have a relationship with someone who is totally capable of dealing with any possible circumstance of my life. Someone who can heal my distorted God-image that comes from faulty parenting, rebellion and from all people. Jesus is unique, he is absolute individuality, the "I AM" saves. Only He can face contrary circumstances, even as Joseph's son. He never backed down from being who He was. The power of being ourselves is the fundamental power of all life and it's better than the power of the world to push and get may way. He has the authority of the Father. That's the meaning of being the "only begotten Son." The Son in Hebrew theology carries the personality and authority of the Father. Jesus had the Holy Spirit, the power of being, and the authority of the Father to do what He had to do. There is nothing in heaven or on earth that could stop Him. This integrity, power to be and authority to do is what Jesus came to share with us. The masculine and feminine are totally one; married. That's the meaning of salvation; the wholeness of the life of the children of God. Salvation is the ability to be me and to have the authority to do that which is lacking among the sons and daughters of this world preventing them from obtaining because of the defensiveness be- cause of their hurt and pain also their lust for power and self-centeredness.

Putting the cork on the bottle is an act of disbelief in God. It is a denial of the foundation of the spiritual life, the openness to truth and the teachable spirit. In Jesus, the door is reopened to that wholeness. We are restored to the possibility of our identity in God. I am. We can say "I am" because we know Him (who is) and we can know who we are because we know whose we are. Our dependency has found a resting place. The son of God calls me forth out of bondage not only the conscious me responding, but my unconscious that may not be hearing the gospel whom is locked away in the dungeon. I have the key to the dungeon, but I must yield that key to Jesus. I must allow and invite Him to come with me into that dungeon to walk with me through those past memories of destruction with His redeeming power to set me free from the spiritual bondage of failure of the two primal decisions, to seek the truth and rest my dependent being on the hand of God.

Those failed decisions led to the illusory, self-sufficiency around me and I became separated from spiritual power and spiritual authority. I fell subject to the realm of the world, the flesh and the devil. John 8:34 says, "everyone that commits sin is a slave to sin." We become slaves to sin because of the fall and personal worlds of rebellion against God. We are captives of defensive dependency relationships with no adequate God. We are dependent on created objects which can not set us free as God can and we become slaves to our dependencies and idolatries. Romans 1:18 says Jesus is the Way. the Truth and the Life. The slave to sin is he who rejects truth and rejects dependency on God, losing the spiritual power for being. Dependents we shall always be, never autonomous. The son calls me out of bondage-dependency into gracious dependency; out of idolatry into true worship. We are the "called out ones," the ekkesia; the Church. As dependent beings, we become aware of who we are through dependent relation- ships, then the reality of God becomes the very foundation of our emotional life. That is no surprise to the Bible-believer, but it's a shock to the contemporary mind because of their self-sufficiency and independence. The abnormality of being rooted in the world is a contradiction of dependent beings that are striving to be self-sufficient. But the person rooted in I Am experiences life in an opposite manner. God takes what (to the world) is deficit and turns it into our glory. Some pay lip service when seeking the truth, but God has called us to walk in the truth. John 3:19 says, "Men loved darkness rather than light because their deeds were evil." When someone turns the light on. we go to a dark corner. When someone lifts our cork or shines a light down into our unconscious areas, we slap their hands and push the cork down harder. We made an "alliance" with Jesus if our mind and will have agreed to open the hurt feelings and memories to the son of God. We can take the cork off to venture down into those memories and let Jesus deal with whatever is there. These are the dragons that need to be slain. We have been given into our hand the Sword of the Spirit to slay the dragons (the lies and deceits), the false God images, bad mother images, and the bad father images which have perverted our vision of God. Until we slay these demons of the unconscious, we will be projecting these images onto persons around us and be unable to relate to them as they really are. But with the Sword of the Spirit, which is the Word of truth, the falsehoods can be dealt with by a deadly blow.

Then old self. whose identity came from those false images, begins to die so that the new self, one's identity in Christ can be fulfilled. To make fundamental changes in our psyches, we cannot depend on an illusory God or a Jesus who didn't resurrect. It requires a real God that heals. If we say that God is an illusion (fraud), there would be no lasting healing for our souls.

A real cure requires a Real Healer. Healthy spirituality is a relation with objective spirituality reality. He was resurrected; Jesus really did come out of the grave. The Christian foundation is based on the reality of the resurrection. We are saved and healed by a Real person, not ideas about Him. We are saved in a living relationship, not theories about relationships.

The healing alliance between Jesus with my head and heart to bring the Good News to the imprisoned feelings and emotions brings change in my life. The victim syndrome brings changes in my life. The victim syndrome begins to evaporate as I find new ability to take charge of my life. I take control of my life and have the ability to make choices and also to have an effect on the world. I am no longer a victim of the circumstances. I can't change the bad circumstances, but I have the ability to face them and have the authority to do what I have to do in the face of contrary opinions. The Good News of Jesus begins an effect in my life. Childing. The fifth commandment to honor our relationship with our fathers and mothers.

We as children, all of us have a choice in how to relate to our parents. We can develop skills in childing just as parents can develop skills in parenting. We equip our children with these good childing skills, so that they are prepared to become children of God. The two primary skills are trust and obedience. Trust of the mothering dependency for security of being, and obedience to fathering for meaning and direction. Building a healthy alliance with mothering and fathering leads to a Holy alliance with God; the opposite of infantile autonomy. We are hurt early in our lives when we are dependent on our parents who are God-figures to us. We may, out of fear, abandon the trust and obedience that's required of a child. Our parents are as God-figures who receive God's image and in turn impart that image to us. When we cut that relationship off, we are rejecting their trust and obedience. We are cutting ourselves off from relationships completely and are shutting down our own connection with life itself without any mothering or fathering at all.

Adam was warned that on the day he ate from the forbidden tree of independence from God that he was a dead man. Parents can be ignorant, neurotic, psychotic, criminal and lazy. Why would God command us to honor such persons? The Fifth Commandment addresses the separation of feelings from relationships to help the children survive when the parents are bad.

It was not for the sake of the parents, but for the sake of the children that our days will be long and eternal. God is saying to us honor the process of being mothered and being fathered to stay in relationships.

God does not require children to believe that their parents are "always right." The honor to which God is referring to is the decision to stay engaged in life, to allow oneself to be mothered and fathered, to stay vulnerable to the power of being and to the authority for doing. God does not want us to say to our parents "I will no longer be mothered and fathered by you," even when it's time to leave their parent's home. God wants us to stay engaged in life because, if we do, He will grow us up past dependency on our human parents and draw us to dependency on and obedience to Himself, the true and ultimate Parent. There we can exercise our childing skills with God. If we cut ourselves off, we put a barrier in the path of God, who then has to find a way through that barrier to rescue us from our self-imposed prison. These barriers lock us into our own ignorance and our unteachable spirits. This is why Jesus said "Father forgive them for they not know what they do." We really are stupid. We don't know what we are doing.

God will find a way. It will cost the son of God the crucifixion. We do not lightly let down those barriers. We will require the Son of God to prove Himself. "If you are the Son of God..." God invited us to, "Come let us reason together." A small child will not understand any of this and will cut off mothering. fathering or both.

Inner healing is one of the Good Parent's ways of reaching down to the broken child within to offer the Good News of reparenting the new birth into His family. Trust and obedience are part of the gift of being a child. If the child has learned good childing skills, then he is ready to receive the grace of God when it is offered in a way he can understand. The Holy Alliance was part of Adam and Eve's relation with God. They had their Spiritual lives fully invested in Him; both their deepest dependency and their sense of authority and direction. It was this Holy Alliance that was lost at the Fall. Adam and Eve did not have their deepest dependencies nor their sense of direction and authority any longer in God's undistorted and obedient manner. The restoration begins with a promise to Abraham; the promise of unbelievable blessings; unbelievable from the point of view of the Fall. God did not have it easy to work with the fallen human race, and the promise did not take immediate root in the mind of the Hebrew people. God rescued them from slavery under Pharaoh and brought them to Mount Sinai not contrary to the promise, but from the direction of the law.

The nature of laws are directed to the conscious mind and to the will. God talks to us in plain language and gives us commands to obey. This is a conscious process. God knows there is a warp in the fallen unconscious which prevents obedience of His commands. One has to begin with the conscious to understand and deal with the unconscious. If the holy alliance is not established on the conscious level, it has a small chance of ever being established. The decision making center of the self must choose God. The natural way for God to restore order out of the world of chaos was to give commands. The law is the first step a "tutor" "school master" or "custodian", to bring us to Christ. Galatians 3:24 reads, "Two covenants." The Law only reaches the conscious and is unable to reach and minister or bring obedience to the warped unconscious. The law by itself brings guilt and frustration as Paul says in Romans 7 he cannot do the right things and cannot stop doing the wrong things. The "ought" brings condemnation because the law cannot change and redeem the unconscious. The law is only needed when there is no communication with the lawgiver. The law points to the real presence of the lawgiver, but the law is not sufficient to maintain a real relationship. What is required is personal openness and intimacy. Grace is ministered by persons, not laws. We must meet the Lawgiver Himself. Grace is able to go deeper than the law because it is personal. Beginning with the conscious faith-dependency relation with God, grace is able to deal with the storehouse of unconscious life.

A gracious person is able to deal with the needs of the unconscious in a manner that no law can do. Paul says that does not make the law evil. Laws are an inherent and Godly part of personal relationships. The laws need to be in the proper context with the Law-giver to become a freedom rather than oppression.

Matthew 5:17, "Do think that I came to destroy the Law or the Prophets. I did not come to destroy but to fulfill." The two highest laws in the universe according to Matthew 22:37-39, "You shall love the Lord your God with all your heart, with all your soul and with all your mind. This is the first and great commandment. And the second is like it. You shall love your neighbor as yourself." He transformed our whole relationship to God through the law.

Until God makes agape love an obligation, it is just another "good idea", which we are free to take or leave. Agape love (taking care of one another) has no obligation about it until the Lord makes it an obligation. Jesus invites us into a personal and intimate relation with Abba. The law is about the family of God where the mothering and fathering are in harmony. The law of God is not to constrict and oppress, but bring our being into its fullness. It doesn't get any better than that. It's life-promoting and healing. The Warp in the Unconscious Dealing with the concepts of the unconscious are hard to understand, but it will help to deal with issues related to the biblical view of human nature. We need to know the difference between the biblical view of inner healing of Christian psychology and the secular and pagan view of emotional healing.

The Problem, Healing and Commonsense

Some will say we don't need inner healing, because we are new creatures in Christ. In Jesus we are already made whole and new. If I have a broken arm and someone tells me to claim my healing, then all I need is faith. So I crank up my faith, but don't get healed. I will feel guilty for not living up to the expectations of the one praying for me. Sometimes biblical principles are often used, but are out of touch with reality. Reason and faith are not enemies, they are friends. We are responsible for reading the Book of Creation and the Book of Scripture. When I am sick and someone says claim your healing because two thousands years ago I was healed, it's my lack of faith if I don't get healed. If I am not healed and pay more attention to their advice than to the truth when I am still sick, I will feel guilty for not living up to their expectations. We may get confused with what God is expecting from us and what the praying Christian expects from us. It could be that the lack of faith blocks the healing, but it doesn't give God glory to say and act like I am healed when I'm still sick. We are called to truth, not wishful thinking. I will know when I am healed and when I am not healed. A lack of faith in God will disorient me in the area of trust, security and obedience which will also hinder healing on a physical level. Doctors know that patients with a positive spirit have better chances of recovery. If my faith is lacking, I can go to God for growth rather than feeling guilty and miserable when someone prays for us and are expecting us to be healed. The same kind of situation happens with emotional sickness and healing. We believe God wants us healed and if we come to Him earnestly, He will heal us within and physically.

There are many born-again, baptized in the Spirit people ministering powerfully and at times have emotional and spiritual difficulties. Taking this approach to healing leaves us with two choices; they are not born-again because they are not healed or deny that the sickness exists. Either option is out of touch with reality. We know that they are Christian, born-again, and if they still have the sickness as Paul said, "thorn in the flesh." The faith question can be asked, but not in a twisted manner.

Why An Unconscious?

The unconscious is the "not understood" part of ourselves (Alfred Adler). The ego as subject to the "drives" of the unconscious, the ID and the super-ego (Sigmund Freud). Also, the objective, archetypal or collective unconscious (Carl Jung). These three secular psychologies started in the early twenty century and in disagreement with each other. The Alder's view is most biblical. From the biblical point of view, some of its material can be used by Christians with profit. The Christian must be careful when using secular sources that they are compatible with the biblical framework. The notion of the unconscious was developed by secular therapist first, for the same reason that Christians try to account for behavior and feelings and reactions that are hard to explain on the conscious level. If you begin with a biblical cosmology, you will have a biblical understanding of the unconscious.

There are miracles where people are healed instantaneously. We can be new creatures in Christ, but there are no "quick fixes" that are out of touch with reality. Some things have to be worked through slowly and painfully. That is not denial of the power of God. Man at One Within. Naked and unashamed, Genesis 2:25, "And the man and his wife were both naked and were not ashamed." This is one of the top ten most misunderstood verses in the Bible. The word "ashamed" as the word "naked" attracts the greater attention. Clothing and nakedness have symbolic meaning. The shame with the nakedness implies vulnerability and impotence. Two persons secure in their sense of identity, their ability to be themselves, with purpose and with two persons whose faith, dependency and obedience relationships were of the highest quality. They could offer each other their gifts of masculinity and femininity while perfectly at one in their relationship. John 17:21 says,

"That they all may be one as you Father are in me, and I in You that they also may be one in us, that the world may believe that you sent me." I pray for those who are sent out and those who will believe in me through their word. This is a unity unfamiliar to the world and something that the world needs. If this joining were to happen, the world would say God produced it. It would be convincing evidence to the unbelieving world that Jesus really is from God, if He could create that kind of unity in and among people.

The Roman Empire was converted by common people that followed Jesus. When a plaque came, everybody would run and hide except the Christians. They would stay and help everybody. One of the Roman emperors who persecuted them asked why do they (the Christians) stick together and help everybody? When a plague comes everyone runs and hides. The pagans saw the unity the Christians had. "If that's what following Christ does for people, I want to follow Christ." They say the unity among Christians was from God. This is true and still has the same effect where Christians are faithful (sold out) to God and each other (The two great commandments).

A common error in reading Genesis 2:25, "And they were both naked the man and his wife and were not ashamed." It was an openness to security, not blindness; a glimpse of the Kingdom of Heaven. The nakedness of Adam and Eve is the openness of soul required by Faith Decision #1- Openness To The Truth. It is more than intellectual curiosity. It s receptivity and sensitivity. Adam and Eve were open to the reality of each other at the deepest level of their being. There were no walls, no hiddenness, no sins, fears or anxieties. No hurt put on one by the other, no betrayal or put down. Being open to life and each other was the faith, dependency and obedience of high quality. They travelled the distance of The Five Decisions to Be Whole and Well. They stood securely on the Hand of God and heard the Voice of God giving them direction and purpose and meaning. Out of that security, they could be free with one another living without demand, giving and expecting no repayment. The external openness and unity within the self is such that no part of oneself is blocked off out of communication with another part.

It implies a complete and fully integrated unity of the self; body, soul and spirit. It implies a harmonious unity of soul, mind, will and emotions so that one part of me is not pulling in opposition to another part. There is a cake on the table, my mind tells me it's not good for me, and my emotions will back up that decision, not undermine it. I will not be seduced into wrong doing because the whole of me; I will be aimed in one direction. That is the meaning of holiness and an undivided heart. Sacramental Unity of Body and Spirit. The Bible is not a "spiritual" book, it's a sacramental book of matter and spirit. Adam and Eve naked and unashamed is a sacramental picture of heaven. It is a picture of the creation functioning as it was meant to function. The physical world is an outward and visible sign of the inward spiritual life of God, the source of all being. "Naked and unashamed" is the earthy, physical picture of that sacramental nature of the cosmos. It is that nakedness that allows the sacramental nature of the Spirit of God to shine through. The opposite of nakedness is not "clothed" but rather a defensive reaction; a kind of protectiveness that humans adopt when not living in the grace of God. The fig tree and brushes of Genesis 3, the present fallen state of the world.

Adam and Eve were two persons able to be themselves and before each other. People are encouraged to "just be yourself" but when we try to be ourselves in front of another, we discover difficulties. We spend a lot of time and emotional energy hiding our real selves from public exposure. The last thing we want to be is "naked." We feel that our genuineness would be rejected if they found out who we really are. We think, "They will not love me anymore." With Adam and Eve, there we no blocks, no hiddenness; what you saw was what you got because the outer was the sacrament. The revealer was not the disguise of the inner man. There was free flow between the conscious and the unconscious. Every part of their inner being was accessible to every other part. This inner unity resting on their foundation in God was what enabled them to be unified with one another. "If we walk in the light as He is in the light then we have fellowship with another" (1 John 1:7). If the center of my being is Christ, if Jesus is sitting on the throne of my life, if God is the upon whom I put my dependency, then I am able to share that center (which is eternally secure). It cannot be taken from me, because my security and my salvation are sure.

In that freedom of the sons and daughters of God, I am able to be fully myself before any situation. It was that freedom manifested by Jesus, the incarnate Son of God who was the final definition of our being made in that image. Such freedom comes from radical dependency upon the graciousness of God, for no other foundation is possible. That security of being is the unconditional mothering love of God. All other ground is sinking sand. It's the opposite of the kind of autonomy and self-sufficiency that comes from secular psychology and eastern spirituality. In the biblical community, worship is our rejoicing over that Faith, Dependency and Obedience relationship. What is the Unconscious? Sigmund Freud. Alfred Adler and Carl Jung. Mystification about the subject of the "unconscious" not because it is mysterious, but because it has been explained with distorting presuppositions. Freud's materialist philosophy interprets the unconscious according to the reigning model of Newtonian physical forces. Freud talked about psychological "drives" in the manner of physical forces such that the ego was the hapless victim of the id (the mass of the unconscious forces which are the foundation of our psyche)and the superego (the "conscience" whose purpose is to control gratification in league with pressures of social control). The conscious is fighting a war on two fronts, battling both the unconscious and the superego to fend off a hostile takeover from either of those two warring sides. There is no peaceful relation between the three.

Jung took the Eastern cosmos rather than mechanical drives as the model of his un-conscious. The deepest unconscious is called the collective or archetypal or objective unconscious. It resembles the Hindu notion of Brahmin; the unformed spiritual substance out of which all things (such as egos) are to have evolved. It is similar to the Buddhist concept of Nirvana. Jungian psychology struggles to keep from slipping off into vague reaches of the infinite void. It also has a constant battle with unresolvable opposites which are by nature built into the system by an uncertain nature of the collective unconscious. Neither the Freudian nor the Jungian unconscious are familiar to us and both instill dread.

The drift in both Freudian and Jungian psychologies is toward impersonality (not existing as a person). Studying psychology makes sense only if the student is a person (in the biblical sense namely) a conscious, rational and purposive being who chooses to seek and teach the truth. We can throw out any theory which turns truth seeking into nonsense. Alfred Adler was the closest to having a biblical view of an unconscious. He was criticized for being much like "those Christians" because he thought in terms of personal relationships rather than drives. He thought of the unconscious as the "not understood" part of ourselves. That part of ourselves which we have not yet understood, but not something beyond us that controls us. Adler was not a Christian and did not have a biblical view point. His psychology made more room for persons in the biblical sense and for purpose and personal fulfillment than either Fred or Jung. His form of therapy was in the personhood of the man.

Relying and Attending - A Distinction Between "Attend To" and "Rely Upon"

We attend to things beyond our own bodies, but in order to attend those things we must rely on other things. To rely on it, you have to "let go" of it. You have to forget it. You are no longer consciously in control of it. The distinction between relying and attending can be found in playing a musical instrument. I can be playing a tune and focusing mentally on the tune, and almost as a different person, watch my hands as they move independently of each other. They seem to know where to go. That is unconscious behavior in a very easy to experience sense. There is nothing obscured, occult, or weird about the unconscious. It may not be fully understood, but it is a very common experience.

"That which we rely upon in order to attend to something else." (Michael Polanyi).

This definition preserves wholeness of our personhood, how we can explain behaviors that are in conflict with ourselves. The unconscious is that upon which we rely in order to attend to something else.

That means that the unconscious is the ground upon which the conscious stands. In that sense, the past is the ground upon which our present stands. The grounded past is the accumulation of all those lessons we have learned. It's the experience of the past that we rely on today.

Education is the conscious programming of the unconscious. Much of what is stowed away is unconscious and long forgotten, but open operating down below deck, like the engines below, of a boat on which the captain depends on. The unconscious is that psychological ground we rely on as we live.

The unconscious is a time saver that extends our capabilities over what we can do with our conscious. Without the subconscious learning process, tying our shoes laces would still be a monumental event even at thirty-years-old. We consciously teach and train our muscles how to behave unconscious.

The concept of the unconscious takes us to the "faith dependency relationship." Our primary faith, our first important decision is about whom or what to trust for our being. Our primary focus of life and purpose for existence depends on our perception of righteousness. To "Trust and obey" becomes important for understanding the unconscious, a healthy conscious and unconscious relationship. Our relying and attending will be modeled on our relation to the Hand and Voice of God, our being and our doing. "Being" before "Doing" The deepest level of our reliance is our ground of being. Our existence is not something we are aware of most of time. We can never be fully aware of our existence, because it comes as a gift. As we try to search our being. we go into the unknown, into a void of darkness. This is always the case if I am dependent on something outside of myself for my existence and security. I will have to rely on that source, and stand on that ground. It becomes partially unconscious. In a dependent personal being. dependency implies the existence of an unconscious. We have to let go of ourselves, let go of our focus on our existence, trusting that our being is secure. We live by grace, by the trustworthiness of Someone who is beyond our control. When we lose that "self confidence," panic and anxiety take over and we can't act rationally and with purpose. Our ability to focus beyond ourselves fails, and we become self-focused. We need the security of who we are or we cannot act. The deepest level of that which we rely upon is the ground of our being. Loss of security of being always leads to salvation by works, trying to be me by what I do rather than resting on what God is already doing.

Mothering and Being

The ability to be me for a baby Is the gift of mothering, the power of being. The mother nurtures. feeds, plays and talks to the infant, and is meditating to the child the security of being. The child is soaking up from the mother's security his own security and his ability to be. Our existence comes from God; the child is unaware of God. Mother is standing in the place of God for the child. She is God for the child. In the womb she is the whole cosmos, she surrounds and aids the child; nurturing the child into growth and sending him forth in the process of individuation.

Mothering provides the bottom foundation layer of the child's "relied upon" experience. In Eden prior to the Fall, Adam and Eve were created in the image of God and filled with the breath of God. Together they shared the full and open experience of life, known only to them as children of God who had not separated themselves from Him. These children of God experienced perfect mothering and fathering both directly from God.

They experience perfect communication with Him, they had a sense of value, encouragement and direction. They knew who they were because they knew whose they were. In Adam and Eve there was no anxiety or doubt about their ability or right to be themselves, for both were a gift from God. Their dependability and reliability were in God. Because of the quality of the faith, dependency and obedience relationship with God, they could be naked and unashamed before one another. They were free to share the very center of their beings. There was nothing that would split their souls with repressed and bottled feelings. No inner tugs pulling them in conflicting directions. they were at peace and totally unified in their inner being.

Archetypal and Concrete

The unconscious is built up in the head, like layers, and each layer is laid in the order of events as they happen in a persons life. The earliest events form the the foundation for the future. They are the most powerful in their effect. The earliest events determine our views and impressions with which new events have to compete. The early experiences set the stage and tone for and influence one's receptivity to later events. A computer disk has to be formatted to store information. Like the person typing corresponds to our unconscious, there can be crashes with a computer the same way the unconscious has conflicts. Current events in our unconscious have to deal with past history that's unfolding into present and future. They are interpreted in the light of those prior events, which has formed our impressions of life.

If I experience mother and fathering as strong, stable, dependable and loving individual, I will tend to conclude the world to be a place to live. Few negative experiences will tell me different. My "space" between the love of mother and the love of father will be secured and I will know who I am and develop secure boundaries and purposes.

The early impressions have a more powerful effect than the later experiences of life that have all that established past with which we have to compete. Early memories become the foundation "first pattern." We draw conclusions from them that affect the whole of our lives.

Objectifying the Unconscious

To objectify means to see as an object as though right before us, rather than way back in our past, mysteriously forming our conscious and upon which we are relying. When we develop unrealistic impressions early on, they are destructive, hard to get at and difficult to change. Not all fathers are "like that" only some of them. If the original pattern we formed is faulty, we will not be equipped to learn or digest new experiences. We will paste onto people and situations and make false assumptions. Those archetypal experiences can be changed, recalled back into consciousness and objectified as particular, not archetypal experiences.

We need to "dredge up the past" so that we can change not the past itself, but its effect on us. We can let dad be dad or mom be mom as well or as badly as they have behaved and go about our lives as adults. We can let go of our past rather than fret about it. This is a reparenting process in which God (the only possible, successful repairman) takes over. That is the purpose of inner healing. Those early layers in the head, are the ones relied upon as we focus on and attend to more recent events at the front layers of our consciousness. Disruptions in the earlier layers are more difficult to deal with than those in more recent layers. We don't tamper with them because more weight of our dependency is resting on them. We do not disturb our foundation when those early events occurred. They were concrete and specific events. As they recede into the past, they become an original pattern because of the dominating effect they have in our lives. When we become four-years-old, my three-year-old self does not disappear. We continue to collect all the years of our selfhood with the latter standing on the foundation of the earlier.

My yearly levels are alive and interacting like the rings of the tree. When it's four-years-old, the third-year ring does not disappear. They may have a friendly and open interaction as with the cork and bottle. The present existence of my past is what makes inner healing understandable. God does not change the past, but there's an effect of the past on our present life and the lessons I learned from those past experiences.

CHAPTER EIGHT: BUILDING SELF-HOOD WITH THE FIVE DECISIONS

Humans are built to be open to the truth and have been given freedom to reject truth and to disobey directions. Infants do not consciously think about being "truth seeking." Abstract thinking that's not understandable comes at eight-years-old. Life has requirements and we will have disappointments to which we have to respond. The deep level of experience is the ground of our being the "relied upon" which requires good mothering.

The first truth which we need is our dependency. Do we accept it, or reject it? The first information is personal information and feeling information. The second, the Dependency Decision determines how we shall relate to being mothered. We will live with a mother in a good relationship, or build up defenses. We answer the abstract question of truth-seeking by how we respond to our mother. As we grow. this issue of honesty gets fleshed out with the third decision. "Do I take responsibility for my actions and reactions? Do I identify myself as one who stays open to relationship with my mother and father or do I rebel and retreat? Do I become a 'What you see is what you get' person, or will I learn the art of deception, hiding and manipulation?"

We become truth-speakers as well as truth-seekers. The fourth decision requires good fathering, discipline, purpose, and direction; all of which support and affirm the rightful gift of mothering and the ability to be myself. I must have built into my "relied upon" self a firm sense of the goodness of fathering which puts the good fathering seal of approval on my identity. If the fathering love, mothering love, and I have experience, we are wedded together and these decisions will be layered into my unconscious, relied upon and I will have the foundation to go out into the world to live on the Kingdom Plateau of faith, love and hope. And if I don't, I won't. My inner identity will be twisted, broken and in need of help from the deep processes of salvation and sanctification.

The unconscious is both rational and conscious. There are two errors; misconceptions about the unconscious that need to be dispelled. The unconscious is irrational and the other is that the conscious may include non-rational elements such as luck. The unconscious is not itself irrational, random or chaotic. The unconscious has a clear logic of its own and is rational. It feels irrational to us because it is in conflict with conscious hopes and plans.

We need to understand the "not understood." Here, Alfred Adler is referring to the unconscious. The unconscious is not itself unconscious. Theories of evolution tell us that the origin of all things was the primal unformed state. We are not to imply that evolution has no place in a theory of how things work, but when it excludes a personal Creator God as planner and mastermind, this theory is Godless. Example: The "big bang" theory or the cosmic substance out of which all things were supposed to have emerged. A cosmic soup or dust devoid of personality, distinctions, or individuality. In ancient mythology, it is the womb of the cosmic "Great Mother." Both the Jungian and Freudian theories of the conscious have roots of this unformed state. Whether the Freudian (which is rooted in biology) or Jungian (rooted in ineffable spiritual substance) are objective descriptions of how it actually happened, it is very misleading.

It does seem to "feel like that" but the theories have some plausibility. The pagan and secular people who are in the womb of the cosmic "Great Mother" are drawn into the unformed state (evolution) without individuality or personal consciousness. It is the state of non-being or death, creatures without hope. The consequence of such a view of life is impersonality of the unconscious, the void, the Pit. the Abyss and Nirvana, will one day swallow us. In the pagan and secular worldview, personal life has no hope.

The Friendly Unknown

Life can become a place of hope and joy if we sense that the "unknown" is a friendly unknown. The unconscious is the repository of much of the "unknown" about ourselves. If the unconscious is unfriendly toward personhood, than our conscious is condemned to float "forever" on a sea of fear and anxiety of Freud's libido (psychic energy) and Jung's collective unconscious. At this point, the biblical view of life differs from views outside the biblical realm. In the non-being or death, exist creatures without hope.

Biblical world life does not begin in an unformed state of cosmic dust, neither physical as in modern secular views, non spiritual as in Eastern mysticism. It begins with a Person, already there, complete and eternal. Whatever exists is called into existence by that Person, the original cause of all things. The unknown part of life the "unknown" is a friendly known and is surrounded and dominated by a Friendly Creator. The "unknown" to the fallen, broken world is not unknown to the Son of God.

Conscious Precedes Unconscious

We do not emerge from the unconscious as Jungians hold. The unconscious is a storehouse of memories of good or bad lessons learned. If our feet are no longer on the Hand of God, they rest on something less reliable than God in the closed-circle of the Uroboros; the cork by which we repress our unhappy past. The repressive pressure greatly distorts our perception of our ground of being because it proceeds from a dark and unhappy source. The unformed state of being cannot explain the existence of more complex state of being. The unformed state requires a God to explain the progression from unformed to formed who is an Intelligent Designer. "Random selection" or "chance" gives an inaccurate answer to the important questions of life. Neither the power of being nor the power of causation can rationally be attributed to randomness or chance. Randomness and chance are the absence, not the presence, of cause and explanation. Conscious life did not emerge out of a prior state of unconsciousness, except for our awareness as individual personal growth. Each of us grows out of a less developed and individuated state of consciousness.

In order for that growth out of our own undeveloped state to happen, there had to be a person who brought things forth whom we can identify and trust. Little babies and elderly without personal care hugging, holding, and caressing, give up and die even if fed and taken care of. We must experience someone, not just things, right at the beginning of life. We are persons who are dependent on others who have to rely upon somethings and are not self-sufficient.

Light At The Bottom

The ground of being in our lives is not Foggy Bottom, but a Person. Our person is not in darkness and void, but light and consciousness. The ground of our being is not a beast coming out of the depth's of nothingness, but the nature of reason, life. wholeness and purpose. In God's world we are not standing over a void, but on the Hand of God. His creative power that holds us in existence and His power of being is the joy of life, a well that gushes up to eternal life. Our being in God is not lifeless, it's the energy and power of life, the foundation of all deep and true joy because we are not dependent on the circumstances.

Maturation and Personal Relation With Our Creator

We need to be "born again." In Greek it means "from above" outside the created order; a metaphysical rebirth. Metaphysical is not being out-of-touch with the here and now of daily life, but a personal relationship with God. If feelings are perceptions of relationship we must locate the source of those feelings of power and authority. Are we trying to receive power from the created order or from God who alone is outside and independent of it? Jesus tells us to build our houses upon the rock and to rest our stability on the hand of God. Matthew 7:24 says, "Wise man which built his house upon a rock..." If God is our ultimate dependency, when the winds and rains of change and circumstances come, there will not be chaos. If our dependency's in a gracious, personal and loving God, there is light and clarity of the presence of God. In the presence of God, I am in whom there is no darkness, no unknown, and no unconscious. The contents of the unconscious are not themselves unconscious, but supremely conscious. God named Himself Yahweh, I Am to Moses in Exodus 3:13. God was giving His very identity. He is the One who has no antecedents, the one who does not rely on anything outside of Himself to be Himself and doesn't have an unconscious. God is the one in whom there is no darkness, only light and is aware of all that is. The gift of salvation, light and glory begin to shine through us from the depths of the power of the Holy Spirit. As might be expected, much of that happens unconsciously as the Light shines into the world around us.

The principle is that the consciousness must precede the unconscious, not the other way around. An infant does not develop a personality unless it lives in the presence of someone who has a personality beyond that which is modeled for him by parents and culture. If I am raised by persons with strong, clear, and competent personalities then I will have a good chance to develop one also. The development of personality by dependent beings comes from another person who is with them; the parents, Who provides the model toward which I will grow and sets a ceiling on how far my personal development can grow?

Two Levels of the Unconscious

There are two fundamental levels; the first is the archetypal (pattern) that is formed by God, the relation to Him, the Source of our being not the Jungian collection of experience and lessons and impressions built up. It is my personal exchange between myself and God and the exchange between myself and the world, of people and circumstances around me. As we are only aware of the world, my exchange between myself, the people and circumstances, this is the foundation of all idolatry. We treat mother and father as though they were God. Our spiritual growth will lead us into the awareness of the primary circuit of our relation with God. Jesus referred to our move into that awareness and the acceptance of it when He told Nicodemus to be "born again" and to enter into a relation of the primary circuit with God. Our relation with God takes place on the conscious level and the unconscious level, a necessary consequence of our being dependent beings. The unconscious level of our spiritual life will always be there because we will not be aware of all levels. You have to rely on your eye to see other things but in doing so, you lose consciousness of your eye. We will not be able to be directly aware of those levels of ourselves upon which we must rely in order to attend to other things.

Keeping Things Together

For the distinction of those things in the secondary circuit which keep one from focusing on the ground of ones being, the primary circuit, meditation is important. Meditation is important in our spiritual life. There are also some dangers and misinterpretations. Some meditations are designed to dismantle our relation in the second circuit with the world around us, saying that the world is evil or an illusion. This is practiced by Eastern religions, mysticism and Transcendental Meditation. God has created the world to be good. It is a sacrament of His Life and we are part of that sacrament. As we grow our primary circuit we are not to dismantle our relation to the world but submit it to Him. That is how our sacramental nature is fulfilled. To dismantle the secondary circuit by persons who are dependent is self-defeating psychologically and spiritual self-destruction. Eastern religions believe that we are not dependent beings, but are self-sufficient, divine sparks. We are not to be persuaded that all religions are "saying the same thing" or "going the same way." The biblical community offers an alternative to the snares and threat of falsehood and darkness. In the healing of emotions, both circuits must be addressed. Both the secondary circuit of collected memories of ones personal history and the primary circuit of one's relation to the Source of being are part of the healing process. In the beginning, our mothers and fathers act in the role of God for us and they give us our first lesson or clue of God whom we shall meet one day. Many of these lessons and clues are unconscious and requires healing and the redemption from experiences that have given false and misleading information about God, the world and ourselves. In God there is no darkness, 1 John 1:5 reads, "God is light." There is no unknown, no unconscious, or total self-awareness. In man there is a dark side; not necessarily evil, but unknown. The unconscious is not evil, but good. It is part of a dependent person. It can become evil, confused and a target of the forces of evil.

When the conscious and the unconscious becomes split, the only way that the dark side of us can be filled with light is with certain conditions:
1. The unconscious has to be grounded with God who is personal and not impersonal.
2. That Person must be omnipotent and omniscient to guarantee stability.
3. That person must be gracious so that we can experience and the ground of our being as a gift.

To experience the dark side as light does not mean eliminating the unconscious. It means that the unknown is experienced safely rather than dangerously. We feel ourselves to be "in good hands." There is still a mystery, but it is a good mystery. The world does not feel like anyone is in charge, it does not feel as if it's going to chaos. We can go to sleep in peace at night knowing that everything is in the Hand of God. I don't have to control everything, I can let it go, I don't have to know everything. I am no longer driven to the Tree of Knowledge of Good and Evil. The tree of universal knowledge and omniscience belongs only to God.

Things are being taken care of with or without me. It's okay to be a dependent person, for my ultimate dependency is God, who is dependable. This is the security in which Adam and Eve were able to stand naked and unashamed. God is calling His whole Creation back into His security. Our awareness is that at the bottom of our unconscious is light, not dark; A person not a void. The awareness of God is a powerful weapon in the warfare against the Kingdom of darkness. One of Satan's tools for controlling us is by fear of the darkness and fear that not even God can handle darkness.

Inner healing is letting God enter into that unconscious area of darkness, confronting it and bringing us into the victory of Light. The Tree of the Knowledge of Good and evil like the Tree of Life is a symbol at home in methodology. The Hebrew phrase refers to universal Knowledge. or omniscience. The Tree of Knowledge of everything from A - Z; The Hebrews would say of Everything from Good to Evil. Our insecurity drives us toward that kind of knowledge so that we might better survive in our unstable world. The flat table is our standard measure. We want to know what is really right and what is really wrong. If we want to know what it means to be truly human, we need to know God, who is the model of human health and wholeness.

Philosophies say all morality is relative, but we have feelings that certain things are right and that others are wrong. Only God can give us an experience of life which will come out consistent and yield a non-contradictory picture. According to God in the question of human nature, He himself is the measuring rod of cause and effect. He is the fundamental experience of the ground of our being, the bottom foundation, the Rock upon which we are built. "That experience of being a creature the effect of a cause is the fundamental experience of cause and effect", (The biblical worldview). To be born-again, born from above, out of the created order is to become dependent of God, to return to the experience of being caused by God.

To be a child of God is the experience of being an effect of someone else who is the cause.

BUILDING SELFHOOD WITH THE FIVE DECISIONS

1. The experience of myself as an effect. The experience of existence as caused by someone outside of myself, corresponding to the primary circuit between myself and God.
2. The experience of myself as a cause. The difference between subjective, in the mind only and objective, real, actual. The difference what I myself cause and that which other beings cause me to experience, both relating to the primary and secondary circuits.

These two decisions define our perception of reality. They are necessary for our common distinctions between real and unreal, sane or insane. They form the basis for the faith-dependency relation and are the foundation for the spiritual and any other life. When I don't want to experience myself as created. the effect of a cause outside of myself is not able to make sense of the biblical faith as a response to a personal creator God regardless of what I intellectually profess. Deep down in my dependency is a pattern of the secular and pagan worldview. Experience the self as quasi personal (as if) and the cosmos as impersonal. The faith-dependency decision to rest my dependency on a personal creator God will seem artificial. I do not experience a consistent distinction between that which I caused and that which other beings cause me to experience. I will be unable to form a consistent distinction between that which I caused and that which other beings cause me to experience in the world between real and unreal. The faith-dependency decision to be a truth seeker will never get off the ground.

Truth testing requires a secure foundation in the spiritual life; the faith-dependency relationship. If my experience of the ground of being is of an impersonal, excluding personal elements as the history of secularism shows. All personhood be not explained, but explained away. An impersonal philosophy and cosmos cannot explain the existence of personal, but the personal cosmos can explain the existence of the impersonal (Personal Empiricism and God). If I experience the ground of my being as fundamentally personal, my search for truth allows for personality.

Personal Truth at the Core of Life

The unconscious perception of dependency determines my attitudes in these matters. In the area of personal stability in the level of doing and moral authority. My experience of a personal cosmos will be opposed to that of an impersonal cosmos. The personal cosmos has purpose for existence with moral order. The impersonal cosmos will not. (Personality Empiricism and God). Stability of being are real issues of creation vs. evolution. The issue is not who does better "science" or to be reasonable. Scientific procedure or investigation can be done by both the un-believer and believer. The question is whether secular people or biblical people have a rational explanation for our ability to do science.

The biblical foundations:

Psalms 11:3 "If the foundation be destroyed what can the righteous do."

Romans 7:9 "It is no longer I that do it but sin which dwell in me."

Isaiah 28:16 "A tested stone a precious Cornerstone, of sure foundation."

Matthew 16:18 "On this rock I will build my church."

Matthew 7:24 "A wise man who built his house upon the rock."

The clear implication is that following Jesus will lead us to the knowledge and experience of that fundamental truth, upon which our lives can safely rest both consciously and unconsciously. The Warp Innocent, but Not Mature.

Adam and his wife Eve. were both naked and not ashamed; a unity Jesus prayed at the last supper while standing firmly on the ground of the provision of God for there being and for their welfare. Self-governing in the 20th century was inspired by the industrial revolution, the conquering of darkness with the light bulb, the conquering of distance with the railroads and hard labor with the steam engine, all undergirded by the new theory of evolution. The collapse of this with the failure of science and psychology to bestow upon us the "good life" with pleasurable inventions of electronics. There are so-called liberals with the false notion of the goodness of man independently of God, whom they want out of public discussion. They are liberals who do not liberate, who don't believe the truth is objective (real, actual) who substitute good feelings for "truth." Conservatives (who don't conserve anything), neither are capable of the vision of God. Adam and his wife Eve rejoiced in being dependent on God because that was the best way to live the fullness of life in all its dimensions.

Adam and Eve desired to be children of God. There was no division between them because there was no division between them and God. After Eve's (and later Adam's) choice to eat from the forbidden tree, they no longer accepted God's dependent relation as their source. Was it rebellion, foolish ignorance or immaturity? Some suggest they were immature. It may be that God had planned to teach them the Way of the Cross (The Tree of Life) and equip them to go to the lost to retake the Fallen World ruled by Satan. But they went ahead of God, being independent of Him before they were equipped to take on the world. God was not unaware how He would teach them the Way of the Cross as His enemies rather than His friends. The Tree of the Knowledge of Good and Evil in mythology pictures the cosmos as a self-sufficient, self sustaining, independent entity. A cosmos with no need of God, a closed system. They hid from each other behind fig-leaf aprons and from God, behind the brushes. These fig leaves and brushes symbolically represent our first attempt to hide from reality. We were no longer able to share ourselves openly and freely with one another. The human race abandoned its secure ground and can't sustain its relationships with the same freedom under God. The center of their life no longer being an unfailing God, that center now needs protection from intrusion and threat whether real or imagined.

Split and Collapse

Defenses were erected which destroyed their sacramental nature. The first defense is against the spiritual center itself cutting oneself off from God, for that center represents one's dependency on the throne room. This rejection of dependency may be against "mom" or "dad" in our lives because they stand in the place of

God in our lives. The first thrust is against being dependent, being vulnerable, manipulative to control the dependency. This inner defense against the memories of the primary parental dependencies. The second trust of our defenses is against one another and the circumstances around us. The defense system is geared to deal with both primary (God) and the secondary (people) circuits with our ultimate dependency on God and with the circumstantial dependencies in the world. Walls appear between soul and spiritual center, walls between Adam and his wife Eve, because of no freedom and faithfulness between them. only "co-dependently" making idols of each other, worshipping the creature rather than the Creator, a love-hate relationship. The matter is confused when we separate from God. The connection with God (primary circuit) and the relationship (secondary circuit) with people, are both broken and can't be distinguished. Our dependency relationships in the world become full of idolatries, preventing us from making that distinction. The effect of separating the soul from the spiritual center is to collapse the spiritual center into the soul so that the two become indistinguishable. The soul tries to do the task of the spiritual center.

We locate our faith, dependency, obedience relationship in the world rather that out of it, becoming creatures of idolatry. Living "soulish" lives rather than spiritual lives, we become of the world, because our defenses are no longer able to be fully engaged. The cork on the bottle becomes a barrier between bowels beneath in the unconscious with the mind and will, above the cork, representing a rejection of the dependency.

The feet on top of the cork no longer experience the ground as the secured Rock, but as quick sand with no stability, holding on to ones own ability to be ourself. We are unable to find a secure place in which to invest our dependency in the world. But even the divided world has some life support to it. When Adam and his wife Eve sinned, they did not immediately die. They lost touch with the ground of their being cast back on their own resources which do not posses the power of eternal life.

They are psychologically and physically alive, but spiritually are dead persons. It's a matter of time before their psychological and physical powers run out and they fall over and look like dead persons. They are like persons who live off investment income, but keep eating into the principle. Without an adequate spiritual life, the spiritual capital (power and authority) erodes away for it is not self-regenerating. We could be as the serpent promised "as God." It can be regenerated only in a living relationship with its source. Fallen man is compulsively defensive obsessed with self-sufficiency and independence. This is the wrong direction to move for the denial of dependency cuts him off from the ground and purpose of this being. This internal split causes an effect on the unconscious layers of "relied upon" material the learned responses and expectations. Because the deepest level of being has been denied, everything built on it suffers. One's whole personality is being built upon an insecure "ability to be me" to create one's own security or "salvation by works." The self has not experienced a free gift from another, it must be secured by what I can do. The foundation is no longer God, so darkness takes over. My existence becomes a question mark, secured by the control I have over the circumstances. Nirvana, an attempt to make one's self "at home" in a void of "nothingness" becomes the goal to be sought by secular and pagan experience. Under our feet is chaos flowing; a sea of fear and anxiety. (St Emmanuel. the Good Martyr) in his "tragic sense of life" being aware off a dark void under him. Once we separate from God, life becomes a desperate effort to create stability on a sea of instability. If the unconscious experience of life is this irrational order or pleasure-seeking will bring peace to the troubled soul. Isaiah 48:22 says, "There is no peace says the Lord with the wicked."

The Pit of Unreality
The Pit into which we Fall when we step off the hand of God, it's a Pit of unreality. There is only one reality created by God and all sin

all rebellion must leach off that reality. It cannot invent its own reality.

Satan told God that he can also make a man out of clay like He did. God said, "Okay try it." Satan picked some clay and began to form a man. God interrupted him and said, "Satan get your own clay." This story illustrates that pagan religions and philosophy theories of evolution came from other stories. The Creation story is original because it comes from God who is absolute reality. The Fall from the eternal foundation was a fall from personal reality and security into a hopeless battle with unreality and insecurity. Driven to the fig leaf strategies, bushes, lies, rationalizations (excuses), sibling, murders, vendetta, and retaliation paying evil for evil.

A Warp In the Human Psyche

In a healthy soul is where we have a relation between feelings and relationships. Those feelings are perceptions of relationships. The damage soul loses connection between them because the damaged soul's contact with objective reality is self-eroding. Relationships become more and more tenuous (not substantial). Feelings take on a life of their own, independent of relationships, living in our own feelings and obsess over feelings. for which persons and the rest of the world are merely tools. The imagination is cemented into the closed circle cosmos headed into narcissism (self love). One's feet are on unstable, unreliable and impersonal worldly ground-of-being whose pull, draws us into worldly processes of depersonalization.

Polarization takes place, the conscious and the unconscious split and our feelings from our relationship are also split three other ways. First in the psychological arena, our inner adult, the independent side of ourselves, and then the inner child. The dependent and needy sides we have deteriorate with one being cruel over the other. The adult in us resents the child side and stifles its expression or the child side is spoiled and runs against the responsibilities of the adult. In the spiritual arena, the relation between the parent and the child dissolves into ignorance, disbelief or rebellion and into the imagination of their hearts.

In the story of the flood in Genesis 6, something strange happens between "the sons of God" and human women. These sons of God fell in love with human beings and had children by them. God is displease and cuts the life span of over 900 years to 120 years. This is a puzzling scripture because there is no historical reason to believe what happened between the "sons of God" and human woman. There is more evidence to show that the human race did imagine such things. The imagination is the image making faculty of the soul, by which we can "picture" reality, even in the absence of reality. When the human soul loses touch with God and no longer has a dependency or obedience relation with God, (who is outside the cosmos) they will begin to picture gods and goddess in the cosmos like the pagan mythology. The search for personal meaning requires it; we cannot stand to live in a world with no face on it. If we don't find a face, we will invent one; a being inside the cosmos and not the being outside the cosmos (God).

These "divine beings" will partake of the weakness of fallen human existence. They are not actual demonic forces, but projections of ourselves on the universe. Sigmund Freud tarred all religion with that "projection" because he did not understand the difference between biblical and pagan religion. In the Fall, we are unable to imagine God as He really is. We imagine God in our fallen image, the reverse of creation.

The imagination of the thoughts of our heart is only evil continually. The imagination is to imagine the truth and the truth we are to imagine is the truth about God. This is what we can't do being out of touch with God, out of touch with reality. We don't have reliable experience of the nature of God. Our imagination becomes dominated by the self-sufficient world living its life apart from God, with no way of correcting its error (sin). Man's primary touch with reality was twisted and warped and no longer able to imagine who God was, which leads to unrestrained lust and violence. The first four verses in Genesis 6 are not historical reality, but of the warped imagining going on in man's heart. These warped imagination about God puts man irredeemably out of touch with God. Satan tries to demote God to his own level by reducing God in the human imagination. God went to the most righteous and notable person on the earth, Noah, to repopulate the earth. Even the most righteous man had a warp on his psyche which will contaminate his family. From Abraham on, the Bible moves toward the coming of the Messiah. God comes into His own creation to deal with sin in the way that only He can. What is Truth? Truth is what is; falsehood is what is not. The warp or fallen nature of the unconscious is the inability of the human race to see reality as it is. Pilate's question "What is truth" was evidence of his morality.

Decision number one. to be truth seekers, can no longer be made. The damage results from our dependent nature trying to rest on a foundation within the creation which was not meant to bear the Load. The warp from the human point of view is unredeemable. I can't be corrected because we have lost touch with reality; the experience of God in whose image we are made. That experience runs to the root of our being. As long as our reality testing apparatus is functioning, we can correct our errors. But once reality testing is damaged then every attempt to correct our error makes it worse. The damage to our reality testing apparatus will also damage our emotional and spiritual lives.

Everything dissolves into relativity (unimportant). Choose this Day; Ground of Being or Foggy bottom. Scriptural reference to the unconscious forces is found in Romans 7:12 20. Paul does not understand his own actions. Its like if some foreign body were in him manipulating and controlling his behavior. "So it's no longer I that do it but sin which dwells in me." Paul is not disclaiming responsibility for personal sin, he is saying it is a compulsive drive toward sin, beyond the personal level, beyond our individual and conscious control. An experience that comes from our divided nature; divided by the wall between soul and spirit by the "diaphragm" between the bowels below and the head and heart above. Paul's personally wrestling his divided and disintegrated self. The product of inner contradictions of his unconscious "relied upon" levels of being. We have gotten out of touch with our Creator and the substitute cannot do the job. Jesus prays, "Father forgive them, they know not what they do." This is what happens in our lives we don't really know what we are doing or what we are missing. Without God, we are missing the beautiful blessings. We are refusing to deal with our deeper, dependent natures. We have a twisted conscious and also unconscious.

The Root of the Tree

John the baptist preached repentance to the multitudes. Many of the Jews, high in rank said, "We don't need baptism of repentance or the new thing God is doing, because we are the sons of Abraham." They said they were the inheritors of all the glory and majesty of the revelation of God. John said God is not impressed with their sonship to Abraham if it carries with it an unrepentant spirit. The axe is being laid to the tree of family heritage, sonship of Abraham; the roots of the family tree, dependency on our past, all the unconscious relied upon layers of early experiences that are stronger and don't let God do a new thing. All of those Godless things that make up what we are. In the Jews, he was going to remove that support they held onto for centuries and replace it with something new. "Repent for the Kingdom of God is at hand." Repent here does not mean God was going to destroy them, it means you will miss the powerful and beautiful new thing that God is doing. John's message was for preparation of the coming Messiah. God was doing something new in human history, striking at the root of the problem; something that would produce a new humanity.

Forward to the Beginning. After John, Jesus appears at Jordan river and tells John to baptize Him, then He goes to the wilderness to be tempted by the world, the flesh and the devil. He returns to Nazareth, goes to the synagogue as was His custom, is handed the book of Isaiah and reads. All eyes were fastened on Him when He said "Today this Scripture has been fulfilled in your hearing." (Luke 4:16). Since the Fall, we lost contact with God; the absolute foundation of the truth upon which Adam and his wife Eve once stood. We tried to replace that foundation of truth (God). In the spiritual throne we tried to replace it with everything imaginable under the sun, (idolatry). The secret of life is Jesus. He is the answer to the distortion in the human psyche on the conscious level and the unconscious. He is the absolute beginning point; the Alpha and Omega. He reveals inner light to the depths of our soul and brings order, not chaos. The sustaining hand of God as a person and not a void. The Good News is that we don't have to live by the rules of the closed-circle universe. We could not find our way out, but God found His way in. The captives and the blind is not just physical blindness its also Spiritual bondage, which is at the root of all bondage. The failure of the faith, dependency and obedience which God is entering in to redeem. "Today this Scripture has been fulfilled in your hearing." We don't know how to pray, because we don't know what the problem is. We don't know how to ask the question and we don't know how to give the answer.

The damaged unconscious is not beyond the healing of God. The hand of God is the foundation of the unconscious. Our unconscious faith-dependency walk can do what our conscious is doing; trusting that God is working below from the other side of our ignorance. We are not alone against an infinite abyss. The abyss is not God; it's the illusion. We need only to do our part, the conscious part of cooperating with God. The rest will happen because God is already doing His part. God is not a cosmic zombie. He is operating at the level of our being of which we cannot be fully conscious. We can understand the activity of God, the things He does and at the same time we may be totality unaware, unconscious of God's activity as it happens in our personal lives. The Spirit of God that comes below our level of consciousness knows how to pray. God acts in and through our unconscious levels in a way that we cannot always be conscious of, but on what we are dependent on, we begin with mothering and fathering and end with Mothering and Fathering.

Letting Go and Letting God

Releasing ourselves to God is this process, is part of Decision # 4 - the blind leap. It is not an unreasonable leap. In our reliance on God, we can't focus on, attend to, or control everything He does because we are dependent and reliant. We cannot focus on that which we rely on. We cannot objectify that activity of God residing deeply in our lives. The difference between resting on the hand of God and resting in the world. (Oswald Chambers) In Matthew 16 says, The Lord makes the disciples conscious of things they are unconscious about. Peter is told, "blessed art thou", and Later the Lord tells him "Get thee behind me Satan." Jesus recognized the voice of the Father through Peter who was a trumpet of the Lord and blasted the voice of the Father. When Jesus recognized the voice of Satan, he rebuked him. (Christian Literature Crusade). Truly. we must "test" the spirits to see if they are from God (1 John 4:1).

Love never ends. When the perfect comes, the imperfect will pass away. Faith, love and hope abide this three (endure). What is the "perfect?" The end of things, like the second coming of Christ, or Christ reigning in glory? The "perfect" is the creation and the people of God, brought to there perfection, the fulfillment of God's original purpose. This is related to "faith", hope and love; the three that endure. The "perfect" scripture itself inerrant without mistakes and infallible; it's never wrong. It's dependable, reliable, sure, and it's doctrine on faith and morals. Perfection is the fullness of the faith-dependency-obedience relation. With that relationship, the essence of our spiritual lives is perfected and other things will "pass away." They will not stop existing, but no longer be as important.

The aids we need to live in the fallen world will not be needed when we are living in the Kingdom and the fullness of that faith-dependency-obedience relationship. We know who we are because we know whose we are. We will rest on the Hand of God and hear His word clearly in a personal, living relationship from the unconscious to the conscious level. The primary and secondary circuits will be complete. If we have built our house on the Rock we are no longer wanders and sojourners in a strange land. We have come home. We belong and have attained citizenship in heaven. Then we will rejoice in what Jesus said, to rejoice that our names are written in heaven. This fullness will come only in the Resurrection. Romans 8:18, "The suffering of this present time are not worthy to be compared with the glory which will be revealed to us."

Isaiah 28:15 Isaiah's prophecy of the coming Assyrian destruction of Jerusalem. They acted invulnerable because of their "religion" they stepped off the hand of God relied on their worldly resources. That was their covenant (agreement) with death, an agreement with Sheol (the dwelling of the dead).

God is laying a foundation for all of us upon which the whole weight of our being can safely stand. The people of God are to build their lives upon it and then that primal covenant with death (first inaugurated when Adam and Eve chose the forbidden tree of the closed circle cosmos) will be annulled and the agreement with Sheol will no longer stand.

When a small boat is about to tip over from the wind, the best thing to do is let go of the tiller and sails and "let it fly." Sailboats are self-righting and will come back up. Trust and obey is built into us by the manufacturer. When we "let go" we will fall into the hand of God. The unconscious responses of trust and obedience take over when we "let go." We would fall back into the law and grace of God. When we are in a storm, we can't manage the wind and the currents. we steer in the wrong direction we don't know how to "let go and let God." We hang on all the harder making things worse because of our ignorant and rebellious attempts. We end up in more chaos, driving the wrong way in the closed-circle. We are too promiscuous (without plan or purpose), ignorant, broken, rebellious, and out of touch with reality in our unconscious area. When we worship the creature rather than the Creator, we do not naturally fall back into the law and grace of God. We fall into the tender care of the world, the flesh and the devil. Life in the fallen world is life without God. We can do some patching up, but in the end it will fail. The only way out of the fallen world is by salvation, being born again, and becoming children of God. We must let God restore in our unconscious, trust and obedience. He is our Creator who can provide security and cosmic authority.

When we are rightly related to God, trusting and obedient, there is a built-in default and natural self-healing process to life. God wants to reprogram into our unconscious "relied upon" as His default setting. When we "let go", we will automatically right ourselves walking and renewed. The leap of faith is built into our consciousness. We spontaneously fall back into the Hand of God and move forward under the Voice of God. The leap of faith is a leap into the light, a leap toward relationships, toward the Someone of all someones. The leap has its intellectual commitments, personal commitment and openness to other persons (not only to ideas). The labors from which we cease in the sabbath rest are the labors of self-creation and self-justification trying to be ourselves by what we do, rather than by grace (by what God is doing).

The law and grace of God are written on our hearts so that "letting go" means a natural return to our Source and Sovereign Lord, falling joyfully into the Hand of God. We should fall back easily and comfortably into the law and grace of God, to the "peace that passes all understanding" when the world, the flesh and the devil have beat up on us.

Life under such substantial conditions no matter the circumstances would be naturally healing. The Light at the Bottom of the Shaft; at the bottom of it all. We will either build upon the rock of truth or we will stumble over it. Isaiah 8:13, "Do not call conspiracy what these people call conspiracy," (plot or plan to harm) to kill the ministry. "Do not fear what these people fear. Do not follow the way or attitude of them nor be afraid of their threats nor be troubled." Let Him be your fear and let Him be your dread, and many who stumble shall stumble there on and be broken, be snared and taken.

Reality does not get out of the way for anyone. In a nightmare, I am in a shaft and there is an octopus at the bottom trying to kill me. This is how our unconscious chooses the foundation of life, an abyss dropping into nothingness, a bottomless mine shaft, inhabited by a devouring monster. In the sanctuary of my consciousness, the enemy wants my will and to deny that there is truth. My fidelity is to the light.

The Five Decisions
1. I will be a truth-seeker.
2. I will put my whole weight of my dependency on that which is reliable.
3. I will be a truth speaker.
4. I will obey the true authority of the cosmos.
5. I will love my neighbor as Jesus has loved me.

What opens the door to the Kingdom of light at the bottom of the shaft is decision number two; I will put the weight of my dependency on that which is reliable and decision number four, the straight arrow decision of Trust and Obey. At the bottom everything is not an octopus, but there is also a loving and supporting Hand of God for His creation and a commitment to live that way.

If in the midst of the darkness we are willing to keep covenant (agreement also like God's promises) and willing to make decision number one in the darkest place, the Light will reveal Himself to us. Reality doe not get out of the way, no matter how dark it gets. When our life is hid in Christ. when we are in touch with the Creator, the world, flesh and the devil can't touch the foundation of our lives.

"The blood of the martyrs is the seed of the Church. The decision at any age to. be open to the truth will prepare one for the light. Our faith will make us whole, perfect love casts out fear," (Tertullian). The gift of the Holy Spirit, baptism in the Holy Spirit, and the Spirits infilling. The Holy Spirit will stop or refuse to touch my will or consciousness if I hesitate and will leave me alone. He will never force Himself inside us. If I stop praying, He will leave. If I don't pray and desire Him with all of my heart, "Thy will be done, not mine." The Holy Spirit will stop before my will and refuse to come in, except as my will would cooperate. This pictures the gender marriage of God. the fathering love of God stops short to honor the mothering love of God for the child. God preserves that "space" between mothering and fathering. The Father wants to accomplish something deeply within us, stops short for our permission, respecting our being (mothering) and our freedom (childing). The God of the Bible treats us with courtesy and respect. The non-biblical world says that we are not worthy of God's courtesy and respect and that God should not demean so Himself. But they are half-right; we are unworthy. God reaches us in any circumstance. The light and power of God. no enemy can touch and guarantees the final victory of good over evil. The biblical psychology deals with our dependent nature; the root of our contingency. The Bible takes what to the world is deficit and turns it to our glory.

Only God can turn our dependency. which the world tries to avoid into that which we must accept. On that acceptance hangs the fullness of our life in God. Worship itself is above all rejoicing in our dependency on and obedience to God, a celebration of the faith-dependency-obedience relationship. He is our God and we are His children.

Our unconsciousness of being mothered. Mothering has to do with being and fathering with doing. In our faith-dependency relationship with God, we let go of mothering (being) so that we can "attend to" fathering (doing). We have to abandon ourselves to mothering before we can fully and freely obey any father. This "self-abandonment" means drifting back of our awareness of being mothered into the unconscious of the relied-upon. We can "forget about it" we have to "take mothering for granted" to be free to be fathered. This is why fathers must call their children forth (wrest them) force them from their mothers into adulthood.

Both men and women must "let go" of being mothered in a way that is not true of being fathered. That is not because being mothered ceases, it is because it drops back into the unconscious and because we come to trust it. We find our being mothered reliable and not in need of being attended to. That happens only when in God we are mothered (loved unconditionally) no matter what we do. That corresponds to decision number #2, trusting the weight of our dependency on God and giving us the ability (not the right) to make mistakes and sin without compromising our being. It is that reliability which set us free to go on to the fathering part of our life mission. This explains why we think of God in masculine terms (wrongly) excluding the feminine. The mothering work of God is more unconscious to us than the fathering work. The mothering love of God is "relied upon" so that we can focus upon God's will. The secular and pagan distortion of gender perverts the whole unconscious process. Our being is no longer gracefully given so we have to scrap fight for it. Because our purpose for life is no longer a given (does not exist), we must get along without it or fake it.

Six Things That Destroy The Unconscious Realm:
1. We substitute feelings for relationship.
2. We substitute the pleasure of feelings for the joy of relationship.
3. We are driven to salvation by works, trying to earn our love and our right to be and do.
4. Mother becomes the both-giver of life-devourer of life.
5. Father becomes someone who is "always telling me what to do" someone to escape, not obey, and authority is reduced to power struggle.
6. All the traits of the Damaged Self begin to appear.

Those six characteristics of the Fall portray our own fallen image. We can be redeemed only by the intervention by the Creator. Imagine Jesus and the Healing of Memories. The Imagination and the Incarnation, Reality and Myth. The prologue to the Gospel of John is the creation story and involves the creation story of the cosmos. Not every scene in scripture is meant literally. There are metaphors (comparing something with something else), But the concept of personhood is a close and understandable rendering of both divine and human being. Personhood is the most literally applicable between God and man. Persons beginning with God are the basic entities (what are real). The secular world cannot distinguish between myth and history or distinguish truth from falsehood, as we try to do. Nor whats relative (not real) or objective (what is true) and real. Secularism has turn God, the archetypal (original pattern) to a myth (fable) out of favor metaphysics (supernatural). Modern thinking of "relative" unreal rather than objective (real) truth. For most philosophers metaphysics is dead (God is dead). Few historians believe that history has an objective moral end, that it evolves randomly according to the current (chaotic irrational) forces at work. Children don't show a clear distinction between myth (imagination) and reality. You ask them is Santa Claus real, they say no, is he coming for Christmas they say yes.

Some people say we believe in the virgin birth of Jesus, but have doubts about the existence of God. Our contemporary world has trouble relating the cosmos with archetypal (God the original pattern) about who is God. God really did enter human affairs on our level. Because the Bible is true we can distinguish between myth (imagination) and Santa Claus and God who is true.

Entering human affairs is not a problem for God because He's a person who called us into being persons. It's a problem to those who find God as impersonal and unimaginable. The biblical religion is not an old fashion. weak, outdated, sect (group that falls away from the established Church). It is how Christians have always looked at cosmic reality.

Incarnation and Reality

The mystery of the incarnation, why He came into the world as a creature. Was the Old Testament revelation sufficient or the revelation by the Spirit of God into the heart of man not sufficient? Why was the Word of God through Moses and the prophets not sufficient to accomplish His purpose? It is difficult for us to imagine God coming to us in our own clothing. He did it naturally and at ease. It was not beyond God's imagination to do it. Philippians

2:5 reads, "Taking the form of as servant being born in the likeness of men." The son of God lowered Himself and thought it was a good idea if we do the same. We can't do it with our own strength, because of our weakness and we are striving to be "as God" independent, autonomous, decision makers. We will not stop until we find a safe ground upon which to rest our dependency and a loving authority to obey. That is what the incarnation is all about drawing us back to the Hand and Voice of God.

The reason for God revealing Himself beginning with Abraham was, we did not know Him as we were meant to. One has to reveal ones self only to those who do not know one. We did not know God personally, intellectually, theologically, or relationally. We could not imagine the truth of who God is, because our imaginations are distorted. Separated from God our imaginations can picture God in ways that are untrue to His nature. the worst is to imagine God as unimaginable. For this God, reveals Himself beginning with Abraham and the promise in Genesis 12. It was sealed in the blood covenant in Genesis 15 through Moses and in Exodus there was the Law and Mt. Sinai, David and the prophets and the Temple worship. It was the growing sense of a coming Messiah, the Babylonian Exile. The development of the synagogue that contributed to the Hebrew understanding of God. All of this talks of a personal and intimate God, this is why Jesus could talk of God being our Father and of our being His children. Jesus came to make God intimately and personally imaginable.

Intellect, Imagination and Story Telling

The imagination in modern western culture is a high priority. The intellect and linear reasoning processes is like a toy or plaything which he will outgrow when he arrives at the age of reason. "Oh that's just your imagination." It is imagination and fantasy. Experience is not as secularist claim to be limited to the five senses. It must include all possible kinds of experience, including intuition, feelings and emotions. Reason is one of our most powerful reality-checkers. It analyzes, takes apart, abstracts and compares. It will test logical consistency. The imagination is our creative picture-making and story telling faculty. It is not just an image-producer, it is a story teller and a history producer. It tends to be historical and relationship oriented. Every person has a story to tell; it is an essential part of being a person. Every person wants to tell his story, to share it with others. That is what relationship is about. In real (relationship) life Imagination and reason must work together. Because the primary entities of the cosmos are persons and persons live in relationship. All relationships need reason. When I become inconsistent and unreasonable in my relationships, they fall apart. One of the characteristics attributed to God is that He is "faithful and true." The world is meant to be inhabited, not chaotic, because the biblical cosmos is designed by God to be orderly. God speaks to us in reasonable ways and we are bound to reason with God and each other. The laws of God are clear and precise for the culture and we are expected to be clear and precise in our obedience to those laws. Clarity always favors truth and unclarity always favors falsehood. Our imagination and our intellect work together to form the inner map to reality which can be a guide for living out our stories. If the map can be shared (if truth is objective) then we can share our stories. Imagination without the intellect runs out of control and is unreliable. We have to check ourselves with concrete experience and abstract (not clear) logic to stay on target. That is true in all aspects of life including the spiritual.

The imagination is part of us. Without it, we would be irremediably disabled. The imagination is an important part of our minds; it's fundamental to our knowing and perceiving functions as is the intellect. The imagination deals with knowledge and the intellect deals with abstract (not easy to understand) general knowledge, making both necessary to a whole human being. The imagination is the storehouse of past memories. Without it we could have no sense of the past. The past is not immediately present to me, I have to "remember" the past. I have to recall it from out of the storehouse of the imagination. The future is not present to us. The only contact we have with the future is to imagine it. Without an imagination, we would have no sense of the past and the future. Only with a past, present and future can we have a story to tell. Our knowledge would be limited only to what is present to us and our knowledge would be meaningless to us because we would not connect our present experience with other experiences, leaving us with no story. The intellect is dependent on the imagination. The imagination feeding upon experience which supplies the material upon which the intellect can work on. The intellect will say, water will freeze at 32 degrees. the imagination thinks, "If I fall into the ice, it will be cold." Experiences involving imagination draws us into relational involvement.

We are particular beings with particular interest and relationships. The role of the intellect is to bring order and reason to our imagination, so that there can be order and reason in our behavior and our relationships. Our imagination as we mature enables us to think and calculate more quickly. We cannot form an accurate inner mental map of reality without the intellect. This partners in managing of ourselves must work together. The imagination deals with real relationship issues not as substitutes or escapes from reality. It aims at obedient relationship not at experiences or relationships that are evil.

God and Gender

The Fall in Genesis 3 is the Fall of human nature out of its faith-dependency-obedience relationship with God into the compulsive, striving after security, self-sufficiency and comfort in the self-contained world. The image of God is meant to be carried to us by our parent's dislocation from God. My parents cannot bear to me the image of God because in them it is distorted. My parents who are in the role of God to me in my infancy set me up for idolatry, defensiveness, immaturity, life in the closed circle, and separation from God. My parents are meant by God to be a delivery system. My father is a delivery boy to deliver a package namely Godly fathering. The mother is a delivery girl to deliver namely

Godly mothering. In their fallen state the package I receive is the image of God filtered through those bad images of God. If my father was cold, distant and demanding then I will experience God in the same way. God has to break through those bad images of Himself as we have to do with one another when someone gets a false impression of us. Our God-images are distorted by the spiritual realities of the world, the flesh and the devil; the unholy trinity. The Holy Trinity of God wishes to draw us in, because there is community within God Himself. Jesus told Nicodemus he had to be Born again from above. The birth image is becoming a child of God and that God becomes our Parent, we become dependents of God male and female. Within God there is something of which makes males and females a unique image.

A teaching on the Trinity, that it is a triune family image, the masculine and principles are with in God and reflected by our own human nature. The Father is the masculine principle, the Son is the child principle and the Holy Spirit is the feminine principle. We need to experience clear images of the masculine and feminine roles in unity which is a reflection of God, which God has assigned to us. Men have the gift of authority to pass on to their children so that they can be the head of their family. Women are given the gift of power to pass on to their children. Power is the ability to be myself in the circumstances around me. Power is the gift of security given by the mother to the child. Without it the infant would die. It is the total security that the mother surrounds the child with, the sense of purpose in life for the child to be what he was created for. The moral foundations are examples of the authority which the father is to convey (transmit). This is not to imply that women have no authority or that men have no power. We are to "major" in the gift specific to our gender and "minor" in the other to resolve the "battle of the sexes." "Reparenting" is a process. Our parents fail to convey (make known. transmit) the gift of security of being and authority for doing. that God wants us to have.

A young woman and the "bad father," as the image of the accuser are a result of sin unforgiven. "The sins of my parents that I am unable or unwilling to forgive will be repeated by me. With revenge, I act out the abuse inflicted on me and my family suffers. I try to get revenge and become the abuser and the abused. I can do to myself what I could never do to my parents. I stab myself again and again because I no longer exist. I want to kill myself. No, I want to kill the abuser inside of me."

Self-hatred comes from a relation from a parent who conveyed negative feelings toward us. The father who has high expectations, in whose eyes, I can never measure up, a father who has no time for me. The self-hatred comes in an attempt to buy the father's "good will." "If I hate myself, then will you love me." Unforgiveness binds her to the abusive father and she is acting out her hatred of her father on herself the image of father within her. It is the internalization of her father's judgement, upon her.

Many are introduced to life by inadequate fathering and mothering. Only God can adequately "re-parent" us and brings healing which sets me free from bondage to those old images. I need to experience power and authority coming from my parents. I need to experience them sharing those gifts with each other. This will provide a firm foundation, so that the child can discover his own adulthood and his own childhood in God. Inner healing aims at reformation of those bad images and to conform to the image of God, introducing the child to the life of the Trinity. Reparenting is being born again, mothered and fathered by God to become a child of God. All emotional healing is being reparented by God.

CHAPTER NINE: INCARNATE AND IMAGINABLE

God draws us into a relationship with Him to experience who He is and who we are. The incarnation is the disclosing of the Father. God looks down from heaven and sees seven billion people focusing on things of the world rather than on Him. We fail to listen, distort what we hear or disobey what we do understand. He saw us focusing on things of the world and thinks "If that is where they are focusing, on then that's where I will go. I will become part of the world they are so fascinated with. If they have tunnel vision and then I will go down and get right into their tunnel, then they will have to look at me." In the Incarnation, God is saying to us, "Now you have to deal with Me directly. No more excuses. You will no longer be able to say, I didn't know." "From now on, if you do not know the truth about me it is because you do not want to know the truth. You will have met Me as I really am, and you will have made your choice." That's the theme of revelation from Abraham on. In Jesus we meet God in the flesh, and there are no more rumors, no more secondhand experiences, and no more theories. Now it's a face to face experience. God becomes imaginable and either we choose "yes" or we choose "no." Our judgement becomes our judgement on our selves. God, who has never been seen or heard, now in their presence seen and heard, in whom they can have life. The Father wants to make Himself known to our imaginations. The Son taught in parables, because it appealed to the simple folk-imaginations of the Galileans and Judeans. God would speak in the universal language of the earth language of love, like a hug, a kiss, a affirmation, a look. In the language of the Spirit, being in the presence of One greater than ourselves.

Personal Relationship With God

Jesus came to re-establish in us faith and a spirit-to spirit dependency relation. He begins by creating that relation between Himself and His twelve disciples. To draw His disciples into a dependency, that will reach far below the conscious level, get to know Jesus quickly, then the part of me below in the unconscious if I have erected defenses and walls will split off my conscious from my unconscious side. That part of me down in the dungeon will not easily be allowed to come into the presence of God, that's the part of me that does not yet believe the Good News. If the Holy Alliance forms between me and Jesus, I can go into the dungeon with Jesus to bring the Good News and to fulfill the Great Commission to my unconscious. The hurting child, the rebellious and bratty child in me, all need to hear is the Good News. We cannot be depended on someone we don't know personally.

If I know only about Jesus, not Jesus Himself, through a relationship then the dependency is not established. When a crisis comes, I will not trust Him because I don't know Him, I've only heard about him. I will turn to the created order, the created object, because I still experience the sustained of identity and wholeness.

The church for twenty centuries has maintained that we must have a personal relation with God in Christ, not just have head knowledge. Head knowledge and its resources is not enough. I am still lost because head knowledge alone is inadequate. It is adequate if we are independent, autonomous decision-makers (as the serpent lured Adam and Eve) "You shall be as God." A healthy faith dependency-obedience-relationship will solve my problem. We are by nature a dependent being a creature.

INCARNATE AND IMAGINABLE

An adequate head knowledge of God (good theology) is a good roadmap, it is important, but by itself it cannot save us from demons and dragons of the suppressed bottled. Only a resurrected Christ who can accompany me into my hurting past can save me. We must know God personally, living in one another's presence.

The imagination has to do with this area of the bottle and bowels, the storehouse of memories and experiences of my parental images through which God presents Himself to me. It's never too late to have a happy childhood. We can go into the Bottle. Much damage to our reality contact is caused when we are young and vulnerable through faulty parental relationships. Because those parents were in the role of God for us. It will take another God-like figure to rescue us and restore us back to a healthy faith dependent obedience with reality, which is why we fall into idolatry. We are looking for that God-figure. If growing up means becoming more "scientific" (secular), then we will be robbed, disposed. of hope or happiness the sad and lonely state of loss or death, and without any true God figure to help us, we will rely on therapists and friends. whom we know not to be God and that and we cannot trust to solve our pain and self-destruction The hurting child buried in us, does not believe anyone can deal with the god-like, bad image figure in us. that is over-powering and hurtful.

It takes a new God to deal with an old one, but the child is told no such God exists. The world knows neither the Scriptures nor the Power of God. If there is no relation with God, there is no hope of healing. We will focus on independence and autonomy. not on trust and obedience. We will be forced to take up the Serpent on his offer "You shall become as God." Be forever stuck with brokenness, of identity, and purpose. There are cases of broken lives that never resolve the dependency and obedience issue that keeps them in bondage. The homosexual (addiction) is told, "That's your nature. Get used to it." A homosexual had an abusive father and was attached to his mother. He never connected with the family and fooled himself that the homosexual life was ok. His sexual orientation was wrong, and he didn't see the devastation it brings on the human body and psyche.

When we are traumatized, we distance ourselves from the offender, separating our feelings from that person and the relationship. We push the unpleasant problem down into the bottle of our unconscious while trying to create a split in ourselves with the unpleasant relationship. Submerged in an unreal world of good feelings to cover the pain and loneliness of that part of me being repressed. The good-feeling world is a narcissistic world (self love, interest in ones own appearance, comfort and abilities) of one's own; a sphere with self at center surrounded by reflections of oneself and whatever good feelings one can generate. Such feelings are pseudo-feelings (fake).

No longer telling us about our relationships. They replace relationships with the illusion of the feeling of good relations, without paying the dues of mutual responsibility. Healing requires that we reinvest our feelings back into responsible relationships, impossible to do without motivation and help from the outside in rebuilding relationship. Out of the bottle the center without God cannot stand.

A case study working with shell shock soldiers said that if the soldiers were encouraged and able to relive the memory of the bombardment, it would relieve the tension and trauma of the event. They would be relieved of the traumatic symptoms. They would no longer be shell shocked. Being shell shocked was the trauma of the bombardment and because the soldiers repressed the experience to emotionally survive the terrible conditions. It was bottle up where it erode and poison their lives.

The Lord has ways of helping people understand their problems in ways that never have been done. It is not just releasing the repressed pain that brings healing, but knowing what to do with it. Many therapists have helped people uncover their trauma, but then not know what to do with the pile of hurt they lay in front of them. The answer is just as with conscious memories, bring it to Jesus for healing and forgiveness to be renewed in the faith-dependency-obedience relationship with Him.

It is one thing to read a book about what someone else has done and to feel at home with the dynamics of the process of inner healing while not knowing if Jesus will do anything. The power of Jesus to bring healing and wholeness to broken lives is real in the conscious and the unconscious distorted areas that have twisted and warped our ability to deal with life. Jesus is rescuing the inner child. Walking with Jesus into one's past history comes naturally to children, because they have imagination. Imagination is there to explore reality.

The Lord told a pastor "There is a little child in you. I want you to find that child and to hold him in your arms." The Lord was referring to the hurting and anxious child within us. The child needs to come in the grace of God and into a relationship with the adult within each of us. The adult side of ourselves can be very severe with the child side by taking the attitude of a big brother toward a little brother who wants to tag along on a date, "Get lost, pain in the neck." We "adults" do not want to be seen with the child in us. The child side of ourselves is the foundation upon which the adult stands. The child can also be difficult, behaving like a spoiled brat; rude and demanding So the adult side needs to be able to take proper authority over the child.

Emotional and spiritual health requires a good relation with the adult side and the child side within us. The adult struggles to come out under pressure of parental abuse, neglect and negative circumstances, who puts the child in the bottle and puts the cork on it, imprisoning the child with those negative parents. The adult in us who, with the company of Jesus, the child in God can set the child free. Child here can refer to chronological child, or any part of my life where I was dependent and vulnerable, such as a soldier under bombardment. If my past is stored away in me like layers, growth rings of the tree, than my past is still with me. We react to that past, part in our lives. God does not have to change my past from it was. Not even God can do that. My past history is not the real problem, the problem is the meaning, the false lessons and impressions about reality which I carry with me out of my past. The God-like power of those false impressions. The problem is unresolved idolatry of parental figures thinking that they, not God, had the last word in the meaning of my life. We ask "why was God not there when I needed Him?" Only God can answer that. God was there with future healing and redemption should I turn to Him. Creation surrounds and encapsulates Satan. In our hurt and resentment, we insist an answer to the hard questions. God has never deserted me and is answering my childhood because God can change that. The whole child in me can become a child in God, and no longer be a child in the world. I can be "born again" into the family of God. I can transcend the negativity from my early life because I no longer receive my security from the world, but from God Himself. To become a child in God is to become an adult in the world.

Laying The Foundation For Walking With Jesus

Opening the Cork means reliving in our imagination a prior event. We must be willing to undergo the threat of that event again. If we allow Jesus into the memory, it is not a disaster. It becomes healed. I do not need to live in the bondage put on me by bad parental experiences. The foundation for my present life has been built over the accumulated years of experience that layers over time. During those years, I successfully built (or not) a relation of dependency experiencing a mixture of good and bad parental images. An insecure dependency can cause deep depression and inner panic from which I can't escape. I need to trace those feelings to their root relationships and to bring those relationships into the presence of God. There is a need to connect the deep feelings of dependency to God.

Pebbles and Drops

If you drop a pebble in a glass of water you can easily take it out, but if you add ink you can't get it out. Some trouble spots in our life can be dealt with, because they are on the surface, easy to reach in our conscious mind and will. Other trouble spots are like ink in water; harder to reach. They are dispersed though life in hidden ways, become part of out thinking and behavior. Most brokenness and hurt are on the surface, they are identifiable events. Then they recede into the past of forgotten memory becoming like the ink and water mixture that are hard to reach. From their hidden place, we draw false conclusions from them such as "all fathers are like that."

Some pollutants in our lives are easy to identify and deal with. We confess our sins, change our minds, get healed at conversion, get a rush of well-being and spiritual growth. The "honeymoon" comes to an end, dullness sets in and we wonder if it was real or just an emotional response. We have gotten out the pebbles and now we have to deal with the ink in the water. We have to deal with the unconscious areas, sins, failures and hurts that are part of our "relied upon" unconscious; the "not understood" part of us. Walking into a memory in the presence of Jesus can heal the hidden secret sins and brokenness faults too ashamed and hurts we don't want to face. They can come into the surface and lifted out, forgiven, healed and made whole.

The Healing of Relationships

The phrase "healing of memories" can be misleading. It is not memories that are healed, but relationships; the parental relationships of mothering and fathering. I need to experience what it means to be mothered and fathered in a Godly way. We don't need to go through all the events in our lives to have healing. That may happen in our final healing with God. Powerful healing can be experienced by visiting certain crucial memories in relationships like the distorted ungodly faith-dependency-obedience relationships with parental or God-like persons that need to be healed. God is the ultimate foundation of our faith-dependency, the ultimate Parent. When we bring our experiences of faith-dependency-obedience into His presence, these experiences of bad parenting can be healed. Certain things need to be in place for healing of a memory. The person going back into the memory must go in the presence of Jesus. The Holy Alliance must be included with the power and authority of the Son of God. The faith-dependency relation is redeemed. As our experiences of mothering and fathering are transformed into the life of the Trinity, we are born into the family of God and come to participate as adopted sons and daughters.

A person being led into a memory doesn't need to be a Christian, but must be willing to walk with Jesus. Jesus walked with sinners and didn't mind. Its alright for a non-Christian to be healed of a memory.

Starting the Walk With Jesus

The healing of memories requires a trust that Jesus is a personal risen Savior; not a myth, not a good guess, not a "Whistling in the dark" but an experience in our lives on which we rest the whole weight of our being (into which we invite others). If Jesus is not resurrected, any "relationship" with Him will be only pretend and will lack good results. The purpose is to introduce someone to Jesus on a level deeper than the conscious. The more I point to Jesus through meditation, the more that person is going to experience the Son of God in the context of that memory.

We can begin with prayer, asking God to heal the damage done by the bad memories and set them free from any bondage. Ask them to imagine being with Jesus at the foot of the Cross, comfortable talking with Him. Ask Jesus if He wants to visit this bad memory; He never says no. This allows the person to get accustomed to the meditation and gives me a clue to his relationship with Jesus. If there is a "no" answer, Jesus has some other areas He needs to attend to before He heals that memory. He may lead to another memory or may want to strengthen the persons relationship with Himself first.

When the person's response is positive, ask "Can you hold Jesus' hand as you walk back to that memory?" The physical touch is important because the child in us understands love and protection in physical terms. The child in us needs to be "connected", not just related, to a person who is protecting and nurturing. Ask the person to keep us in touch. Describe the situation, the person there, the scenery, and the emotional atmosphere. The key to the healing is the person's willingness to entrust their feelings and emotions. If there is fear, say "Can you share that with Jesus? Tell Jesus how you feel and how you perceive the situation." Encourage the person to stand close to Him and hold His hand. Ask "How does Jesus respond to what you said? Does Jesus seem disturbed or upset by this scene?" The damaged soul gains strength by living in the presence of one who is not damaged or by the experience of putting hatred down and can be Himself in front of threatening powers of destruction that are present. The goal is to open up and follow clues to the positive and negative energies at work. The person is able to share these feelings in the situation with Jesus, it will open up the person to sense Jesus feelings about that himself. The person discovers that the unconditional love of God in Christ is not quenched, diminished, dented or thwarted by the threatening persons or circumstances. Jesus, the child in God, is the adult in the world. Jesus, the I Am, is able fully to be Himself because He is the "I Am." Therefore, I can be also. That is the meaning of the faith- dependency relation.

Transferring Dependency

In order for Jesus to accomplish His work with His disciples, He had to draw them into a dependency relationship with Himself. Only as they came to trust Him with their being and obedience could He do His work in them. When He announced on the cross it is "finished" the same is true of all of us in our redemption and healing. In meditation, the presence of Jesus draws the child in person into that dependency relation with Him which is necessary for the healing to happen. In doing so, the person's dependency is withdrawn from the threatening figures or situations. Healing requires that the person be able to objectify the person who hurt him by saying "This is just another person like myself; one person among many. This is not God. This is not someone upon whom I must depend for my being or permission to live." In order to objectify that person one's deep dependency must be withdrawn from them. To withdraw from it, it must be put somewhere else. The only safe place is in the Hand of God. This is why Jesus came to live with us. Jesus came to draw our dependency upon Himself through the crucifixion, resurrection and the ascension and to connect us to the Father who lives outside of the circle of creation. Jesus replaces whatever is sitting on the throne of my spiritual center. He becomes the one who will educate my mind, discipline my will and integrate my feelings, emotions and relationships.

Wimpy Jesus

Even if Jesus is there in the scene, during the meditation and nothing different is happening, ask yourself "Does Jesus being there make any difference to the scene?" If not, back up and examine the person's relation to Jesus and perception of who Jesus is. The Jesus some people believe in cannot save anyone unless He draws them to Himself. If this is evident in the meditation, go back to Scripture "How would this scene be different if Jesus really were there as the King of kings and Lord of lords; the risen and resurrected Christ the Jesus of Scripture."

People need to be given permission or encouragement to believe in such a Christ. When they can allow that Christ into their memories, things begin to change. The Son of God cannot come into a situation and have nothing change. If the change is not happening, there is a block between the person and Jesus which prevents Jesus from being effectively present. That block must be searched out. It might be unbelief, unconfessed sin, buried anger against God or anything that keeps one from an open and trusting relation with Him. "What difference does Jesus make to the scene?" is the question which must be asked over and again in the healing process. The difference in the behavior of the other person in the scene, also in the difference in person, him or herself. I need my parental images changed and I need my child (self) image

INCARNATE AND IMAGINABLE

changed also to conform to the image of Jesus, the child of God. Therapy must include the challenge to my own moral and spiritual growth and being free from the behavior of other persons. We need to encourage others to say "Would I behave any different if Jesus were personally here today supervising my spiritual progress? Would I submit to His authority and trust his saving power? In this situation of stress, would I be willing to do it His way?" Only Jesus can lead me into being a secure adult in the world. If the Jesus who "shows up" is not the King of kings and Lord of lords, if Jesus is incapable or unwilling to be Lord and savior, we must back out and find out why the person imagines Jesus that way and help him discover the real Jesus the Jesus in biblical history. The resolution may lie in asking "Do you know any reason why there might be such blocks?" or "Is getting closer to Jesus where you want to go?" or "How would you feel if Jesus walked into this room right now?"

The Healing - Three Sets of Parents

As the scene progresses, keep the contacts flowing between Jesus and those persons present who had an emotional impact. Ask "Does your father know that Jesus is here?" If not, then "Would Jesus like to be introduced?" In the meditation the client perceives between his parent or whoever hurt them and Jesus. Sometimes there is a clear openness and spirit of repentance and willingness to be healed. I changed on the part of the parent figure. Sometimes there is resistance. There are three different "parents" involved:
1. The natural parent
2. The parental image stamped in onc's heart by human parenting; and
3. God, the heavenly Parent

The parental image in the heart is intended by God to conform to Himself in whose image we are made. It is our parents task to convey that image to us by accurately introducing us to God. The failure of that communication is because of the Fallen world and the conclusion by the Lord that the "wickedness of man was great and the imagination of the heart was evil." (Gen. 6:5). Man could no longer imagine who God was without distortion. In the inner healing meditation, it is the parent within that God is dealing with our distorted parental images, not the literal human parent. Changes in the flesh parent are between that parent and God. The client must be willing to set the parent free to have his or her own relation with Jesus. The human parent is taken down from the God-pedestal and becomes no longer the parent, but a brother or sister; a peer. The parent within is an archetypal image made up of many experiences of mothering and fathering. It is one of the primary God-images by which God communicates Himself through us. It is that distorted God-image by which Jesus is here redeeming, not the human parent in that God-role. To do that, God will have us see that parent through His eyes. We will be asked to see that parent in terms of their sins and failures and in terms of that perfect image of fathering or mothering which they are being called as creatures of God. Have the client imagine himself as a fly on the wall, listening to the parent and Jesus in which Jesus reveals to the parent how truthfully and lovingly to deal with the child. Ask how the child feels listening to the conversation and if the child in Him can imagine such a transformation in the parent.

Once the person can understand this distinction and can imagine the parental image as reformed and healed by Jesus. Ask them to rerun the scene with the new parent to experience what it would have been like had the parents behave in a Godly way. The person can receive from Jesus the experience of a father who reflects the heavenly father and can receive from Jesus the experience of a mother from the Holy Spirit. When we imagine our parents being a good father and mother, which is what God wants us to have then the gift of good parenting, it is God's gift to us, not our parents gift, then we can let our parents go with all their failures. We are able to let them be themselves. I am not in bondage to their failures. Their behavior towards me no longer determines my identity, I move my dependency (my childhood) from them to God. We get the experience of a good father because Jesus is introducing us to His heavenly Father, John 14:6 "no one comes to the Father but by me." My human parent may or may not respond to God's call to be perfected in. His image, and that's their problem. I am free to be myself in Christ because my life is hid in Christ. My identity in Christ makes me a child of God, an adult in the world, capable of loving my parents who are stubborn, hard to handle and deal with, defiant in opposition and unruly.

Sanctification

In inner healing, it is important to bring into submission to God those parts and areas that will not respond to salvation and to the preaching of the Gospel. The power of the Holy Spirit is the power to be ourselves; it's the power upon which all else is built. As I receive the mothering gift of God coming through the Holy Spirit, my spiritual journey into maturity begins to run more smoothly. Being baptized in the Holy Spirit brings with it that power of being which the world does not have and cannot give to me. That power of being alone can lead to eternal life. The unity between salvation and sanctification. Oswald Chambers said, "Salvation and sanctification are not separated, they are separable in experience." Being in Christ is sanctification, an impartation of His very life. Being born again and being identified with the death of the Lord Jesus is that His blood may flow through our mortal body. There are two sides of the Atonement. It is not only the life of Christ for me but His life in me for my life. "His life" in me is facilitated by the healing of memories.

The Possible and The Real

Allowing the good parent to emerge in my consciousness allows God to impart (convey) to me the living experience of being fathered and mothered. I cannot by my imagination create that good mothering and fathering nor by my imagination create the presence of Jesus. But I can allow myself to explore the possibility of those things happening. Emotional bondage is not being able to imagine even the possibility of good things happening to us. If I cannot imagine the possibility of something then I am blocked from receiving it. We cannot imagine the possibility because of ignorance (no one ever told us) or because of feelings of self-condemnation and unworthiness (God would never do that for me). We need to be given permission to imagine such goodness in our lives, a permission which the counselor or therapist can convey.

Once we are free to imagine the possibility of a good parent then God is able to grant us the reality of a good parent, good parenting is the gift of God, not of our human parents. Our human parents are temporary stand-ins for God, whose children we are all called to be. In our healing Jesus is saying, "Let me introduce you to my Father through your father." We arrived at a painful memory the first time without Christ at our side feeling alone and impotent. It is like being beaten up by the neighborhood gang, and returning with our big brother. With our big brother we can handle the memory and resolve all of the relationships we confronted. Three Healing Events. Many things need to be worked out in relationships.

Is the person willing to let Jesus be the Risen Son of God right in those circumstances. In the scene when the person responds to the presence of Jesus, things will begin to work out. Repentance will take place. Parent and child will be restored to one another. As the resolution comes ask the person, "Can you receive from Jesus this new parent as His spiritual gift to you so that the child in you, can now live with this parent rather than the old one?" As the person receives this new parent as Jesus gift he is set free from the bondage. The person has to cut the root of bitterness by forgiving the human parent for not having been able to be that perfect parent that God meant him to have.

The client must speak the words of forgiveness. The person must ask the parents forgiveness for any grudges and bad feelings against the parent, speaking words of repentance. Any root of bitterness must have the axe laid to it. Forgiveness needed for the security of the healing, any unforgiveness gives ground for forces of darkness to work again and holds the person in bondage to the thing that is damaging him. the bad parent image. The offending person need not be the literal parent. It may be any person we are dependent on or by whom we perceived hurt. We have talked about parental images the fathers and mothers we all have had. The same principles apply to any situation where we have experienced vulnerability and dependency. This man lost his girlfriend, his goal was to put the whole weight of his being on God.

That woman had been a channel for God to bless him. He needed to ask God what memories he could keep of her and what to let go. He could keep her beauty and grace, warmth, receptivity, softness and her personal strength. This were God's personal gifts to him through her and when she left. that gifts did not need to leave with her. He need to repent for the sex that is only allowed through marriage. But his to keep was that love of God for which the woman had been a channel. That was God's spiritual gift to him. She had been ministering to him feminine gender grace, giving him what was lacking and helping to fulfill his place in life.

Every person important to us carries a part of divine image into our lives. Its part of our maturing to receive that inner spiritual gift from God and then to let go of that person to be himself. The person is a channel, not the source. The healing comes as we see that person through the eyes of God in terms of His plan for that person in our lives.

The Long Ago Good

Emotional and spiritual recovery requires that we allow God to transform past joys and successes and deviations. We've been blessed not deserted. Out of self pity we refuse to be aware that He has given us life. We don't thank Him for these blessings, but instead idolize something of the world. Giving thanks to God for the good things removes those things off the throne of our hearts and places God on the throne.

Acknowledging Him as Creator and Sovereign over our whole life the good and the bad, the pleasant and the painful. To return to the good times of our lives to give Him thanks will help anchor the healing of our past. Only then are we free to deal with the changes of life, because the whole of our lives is then being invested, where neither moth nor rust consumes and where loved ones no longer break our hearts by betrayal or by disappearing. This is not saying that we we are not affected by the pain and hurt in a callous and insensitive way, but rather than we can no longer suffer the damage to our souls that dependency relations bring. We can move through these changes, work through the hurt, and come out stronger than we went in while rising above the fallen world that tries to undermine our joy. As we begin to see all of our dependency relations, past, present, and future through the eyes of God (our ultimate dependency), the rest falls into place in a way that sustains health, maturity and freedom. We learn to walk on the face of the earth, no longer as dependents of our circumstances, but as sons and daughters of God.

Metaphysical Grace

Western culture including churches are cut off from the grace of God the only solution to their problems. It's suicidal to have a wall of separation from the real cure. When there is nothing available we turn to falsehood as a temporary fix. Neither God nor His grace abandons us. The power of being is always waiting to well up to eternal life. We need only turn to God. Our deepest symptoms cannot be healed by changing the circumstances around us. The deepest hurts will not change by what we can do to change our circumstances, no matter how good our behavior. The deepest healing will always come "from within." Not from the Hindu's that claim we are divine with inner divine resources, but God who is separate from me is ready to recover me. That is the difference between the biblical and the fallen closed-circle sense of metaphysical outside, not the spatial or physical outside. Jesus' words to Nicodemus about being "born again" JH. 3 and to the woman at the well about living water welling up to eternal life JH. 4, are about metaphysical reality. Grace like love is metaphysical, not circumstantial. Grace comes from substantial being, not circumstantial being. Until we discover ourselves to be of the Father (not of the world) we cannot be successfully (gracefully) in the world.

Psychiatric Medications lead to addiction. the medication used as a "crowd control" then for healing medications do not heal root problems in broken relationships and memories. They only alleviate symptoms and mask the root cause from the consciousness of the patient so that being in touch with feelings, emotions and root relationships is difficult. The use of modes such as inner healing can be made more difficult.

www.ingramcontent.com/pod-product-compliance
Lightning Source LLC
LaVergne TN
LVHW051601070426
835507LV00021B/2698